Derbyshire Children at School 1800-1900

Dear Mother

     I am as well as anything.

My barth night is on friday. I have got my remove in french. & arith. And I my new dormitory better than. the old one. Football begins on monday—

    With love to all

       Your loving son

        George

A letter home from George Strutt at Elstree School, September 1890. The portrait was taken in 1892, soon after he entered Harrow *(from Elstree archives)*

DERBYSHIRE CHILDREN
AT SCHOOL
1800-1900

E.G. POWER

Scarthin Books
Cromford
2004

Published 2004
by Scarthin Books of Cromford, Derbyshire
© 2004 E.G. Power

website: http://scarthinbooks.demon.co.uk
email: clare@scarthinbooks.demon.co.uk

Design by
Elisabeth Stoppard and Mike Susko

Typeset by
Techniset Typesetters, Newton-le-Willows, Merseyside

ISBN 1 900446 06 5

Printed by Bell & Bain Ltd, Glasgow

Contents

Acknowledgements

To Dr. Margaret O'Sullivan, County and Diocesan Archivist for permission to quote from numerous family records and to the staff at the Record Office, whose high level of professionalism has made research more of a pleasure than a task.

To the archivists of Charterhouse, Elstree and Winchester for their assistance in providing and finding illustrations.

The cover illustrations are from the archives of Scarthin Books.

An annotated copy of this book will be made available in the Record Office, Matlock as soon as possible after publication.

Introduction

It would be unhistorical to attempt to write an account of Derbyshire Children at School as a single uniform topic. To deal separately with The Rich and The Poor might be regarded in some circles as not "politically correct", but it is certainly historically appropriate.

For this reason the subject is here treated in two separate parts and readers may make their own comparisons if they wish. The first part deals with the education of the children of wealthy parents. Schools for such children had been available for four or five centuries before 1800. The education of poor children is dealt with in the second part of the book, not because it was of less importance but simply because it came about later and, therefore, in some respects, derived ideas and procedures from the practices of the long-established, so-called, Public Schools.

A list of the schools and the families mentioned in the text follows. More detailed information on the wealthier families may be found in the companion volume, Derbyshire Children at Home.

School: A view of the interior, looking West *(from Hawkes: Winchester College)*

The Schools and the Scholars

PART 1: Schools for the Rich

Bromsgrove
John Lace – related to the Longsdons of Little Longstone.

Bubnell Hall
Harriett Wager – daughter of William Wager of Great Longstone.

Charterhouse
The FitzHerberts of Tissington Hall.

Elstree
George Strutt – grandson of Jedediah Strutt, mill owner.

Eton
The Arkwrights – grandsons of Sir Richard Arkwright, mill owner.

Harrow
FitzHerberts, Turbutts and George Strutt.

Risley
D'Ewes Coke boys.

Wellington College
Harold FitzHerbert.

Winchester
Anthony FitzHerbert.

Wirksworth (Miss Stubbs)
Elizabeth Bradshaw.

Other Schools mentioned:

Abbotshulme
Bakewell: Bridge House and Church View
Darley Dale: St Elphin's
Easingwold
Marlborough
Repton
Shrewsbury
Southwell

TOYS AND THEIR TEACHING.

Lady Customer. "My little Boy wishes for a Noah's Ark. Have you one?"
Toyman. "No, M'um, no. We've given up keeping Noah's Harks since the School Boards come in. They was considered too Denominational, M'um!"

PART 2: Schools for the Poor (surnames only)

Belper Pottery Boys
> Hardy, Milward, Oliver, Spencer, Stone, Taylor, Wain, Whewell, Wood.

Brimington Common
> Hayes, Neale, Nottingham, Yates.

Kirkstead Girls
> Hancock, Hand, Riley.

Melbourne Infants
> Crane, Paxon, Robey.

South Normanton
> Rowe.

Other Schools mentioned:

Denby Free
Eckington
Evans' Mill School, Darley Abbey
Pinxton Boys
Strutts' Mill School
Tissington
Trowell Free
Youlgreave

PART 1: Schools for the Rich

Choosing a School

> I found Shrewsbury did not answer for Eddy he could be as idle as
> his heart's desire so I removed him to Bury the head Master is a
> friend of mine and most highly recommended particularly for the
> art of whipping little boys – there is nothing to be done without it.

– Thomas Rooper to Sir Henry FitzHerbert on the matter of choosing
a good school, 1829.

Costs and Benefits

In the 18th century the question might not be "which school?", but
"school or private tutor?". In 1793 Lady Sarah FitzHerbert asked her
brother William Perrin for some advice. He declared himself
"...pleased with the hint you once threw out of putting Anthony &
his youngest Brother to Eton... This is the Plan I should undoubtedly
pursue ... if they were my own & this the more willingly as I happen
to be acquainted with both the Eton Masters". For George, intended
for a naval career, he recommended "a year or two as a Parlour
Boarder with Mr. Cherry at Maidstone" to learn mathematics and
navigation.

A month or so later he wrote again. "My own opinion ... is decisively
for public Education ... the principal Benefit ... is derived from
sending Boys there early & keeping them always at one & the same
School". And he went on to suggest the advantages of Winchester:

> The Master has just been changed & most if not all the bigger Boys
> sent away: New Brooms sweep clean & great Circumspection may
> be expected at the turning over what may well be called a new Leaf
> there.

(He was referring to the "mutiny" at Winchester College in 1793).

Like a careful mother, Lady FitzHerbert made further enquiries and,
in January 1794, she had a reassuring letter from a lady who actually
lived in Winchester:

> The Head Master ... selected upon the resignation of Dr. Warton last Summer, soon after all the disturbance in the College, is Mr. Goddard, a man of about thirty-eight years of age ... the next Master or Usher is Mr. Gabell... There are besides two assistant masters.

The total number of pupils, she said, was about 115.

Sarah's correspondent went to list the various fees which had to be paid on entrance, such as six guineas to the masters and three guineas to the House, as well as annual charges of thirty pounds for board and fourteen guineas for teaching. Instruction in Music, Dancing and Writing by visiting masters was extra. She also assured Sarah about her son's well-being:

> I think with Mr. Perrin that the Scholars will be under a much greater degree of Subordination in future ... as the great Boys were sent away, the present Scholars are almost all little Boys... I don't think there are many older than Anthony.

So Anthony did go to Winchester and his uncle visited him there in April 1794, reporting to Sarah that he "is perfectly well & seemingly satisfied with his Situation..." (and Half a Guinea better off as a result of his uncle's visit).

Terms and Conditions

A few years later, in 1797, Erasmus Darwin, M.D., F.R.S., of Derby, the grandfather of the more famous Charles Darwin, published his Plan for the Conduct of Female Education in Boarding Schools, and at the end of the book added a short note recommending the school in Ashbourne run by the Parker sisters.

Their house, he wrote, had "a prospect of Sir Brooke Boothby's park" with a walled garden and a stream "which may sometime be converted into a river-bath". The building included "an ample school-room, and an ample dining-room, and four smaller parlours ... with two stair-cases one of which is of stone". (Reassuring, in case of fire). The house was well-lit and airy and "contains about thirty pupils without being crowded".

Those who were attracted by these features could read on to discover whether they could afford to pay for them.

	£	s	d
Board for a year	18	18	0
Entrance	2	2	0
Tea, if required, per quarter		10	6
Washing, per quarter		14	0
Geography, per quarter		10	6
French, Music, Dancing and Drawing,			
each per quarter	1	1	0
Entrances [for the above]	1	1	0

Pupils had to give a quarter's notice on leaving the school or pay a quarter's board. Another requirement was: "Each young lady ... to bring one pair of sheets, two towels, a knife and fork, and a silver spoon".

Among the advantages of education in school instead of at home, Dr. Darwin noted that children tended to imitate those a little older than themselves, and would have more role models in school. He also explained that children "take pleasure in teaching each other... At boys' schools I have often observed that the lower classes have learnt more from their school-fellows of the higher classes than even from their masters".

The terms at the Miss Parkers' establishment in Ashbourne may be compared with those at a private school for boys in Southwell, Nottinghamshire, in 1789. Sir William FitzHerbert obtained the details from the Headmaster:

> For Board & Education in English, Greek & Latin £20 per Ann.
> Entrance 2 guineas
> Young gentleman washed out at 8 shillings per Quarter.
> A Writing Master attends the school twice a day whose terms are
> 6 shillings per Quarter. Dancing &c at the usual terms.

He went on to ask, "...that we might have some little notice – we have now fourteen young Gentlemen, and have had application for two more".

Sir William, wisely sceptical about unsubstantiated claims, made further enquiries and had reassurance from his informant, H. Rooke, on 23rd June 1789:

> The School at Southwell has a very good character. I have talked to

MISS FELLOWES,

No. 38, BROMPTON ROW,

RECEIVES TWELVE

Young Ladies,

Who are treated with Parental Kindness, and the greatest Attention is paid to their Morals and Improvement.

TERMS:

Pupils entering under TWELVE Years of Age, to commence and continue at *Forty Guineas* per Annum; above that Age, *Fifty Guineas.*

MASTERS, OF THE HIGHEST EMINENCE, ATTEND ON THE USUAL TERMS.

A Quarter's Notice will be expected previous to the Removal of a Pupil, or the Payment of a Quarter's Board required.

Washing, Six Guineas per Annum.

☞ *Settlement of Bills Half-Yearly.*

several people about it, and they all say that Mr. Jackson is a very good natured man and very attentive to the education of his pupils, & that Mrs. Jackson is equally attentive to their health and cleanliness.

A generation later, in 1819, Sir Henry FitzHerbert wrote to Mr. Chapman, one of the House Masters of Charterhouse School in London, about his two sons, William and Richard. Mr. Chapman replied that he would "be happy to take them under his care, and will not fill up his vacancies until he hears again from Sir Henry". A printed schedule gave details of the various fees and extras:

ANNUAL	£	s	d
Board	45	0	0
Schooling	12	12	0
Assistant in the Boarding House		10	6
Writing, Accompts, and Stationery	3	3	0
Washing	2	2	0
Servants	1	1	0
School Groom, Fire, &c		10	0
Seat in the Chapel		5	0
	£65	3	6

N.B. A Quarter's Notice is required on the Removal of a Scholar; or a Quarter's Board must be paid.

	£	s	d
ENTRANCE	12	12	0
Mathematics quarterly		1	1	0
French quarterly		1	1	0
Drawing quarterly		1	1	0
Dancing quarterly		1	1	0
Entrance to the above	1	1	0
Single Bed, if required	5	5	0

The linen to be brought by each boy is as follows:
Eight Shirts
Six Pair Worsted Stockings
Six Pair Cotton Stockings
Six Pocket Handkerchiefs
Three Night Shirts
Three Night Caps

Sir Henry was satisfied with these terms and both boys did go to Charterhouse. Not every well-off parent would cheerfully have met the expense of school and the added expense of travel there and back three or four times a year. D'Ewes Coke of Brookhill Hall, near Pinxton, noted in his Diary for 1817:

3rd September.

> Met Mr. Mason of Calver in Bakewell with his sons who were going to Repton School – he says the expence is about £50 per Ann.

In July 1818 he wrote to his eldest son, D'Ewes, who was then a pupil of Rev. F. Hodgson, Bakewell:

> I send the particulars of the Military College [Sandhurst] for Mr. Hodgson to explain to William [his second son]. It will be so expensive I almost repent I have agreed to send him, & he is so backward I am afraid they will not have him.

Another consideration in choosing a school was health. Thomas Rooper, a friend of Sir Henry FitzHerbert, wrote in a letter of 15th December 1825, complaining of Charterhouse School, then in London:

> William [his son] is better but by no means stout. The Charter House always disagreed, but for that circumstance I would gladly have continued him there six months longer... I hope your youngest boy will [become] inured to Charter House air.

In July 1826 he returned to the subject. "We are thinking of sending Eddy our youngest boy to Winchester, I am afraid of the Charter House air for him he is not very strong". In the event he changed his mind, for the following year he wrote, "...yesterday Eddy went off per coach to Shrewsbury ... there are three hundred boys but they are well taken care of". But fresh air was not the only feature to look for in a school. In March 1829, writing again to Sir Henry, Thomas Rooper admitted:

> I found Shrewsbury did not answer for Eddy He could be as idle as his heart's desire so I removed him to Bury   the head Master is a friend of mine and most highly recommended particularly for the art of whipping little boys – there is nothing to be done without it.

Health and Safety

One question on which mothers particularly needed reassurance was that of care. Mrs. Jackson's attention to the "health and cleanliness" of little boys was a strong selling point for her husband's school in Southwell in 1789. At Charterhouse in 1826 the FitzHerbert boys had a change of Housemaster, but their parents were assured that:

> ... the care and attention paid to all the pupils in Mr. Churton's House, by Mrs. Jeffkins who superintends it, is too well and too generally known to require anything to be said in her recommendation.

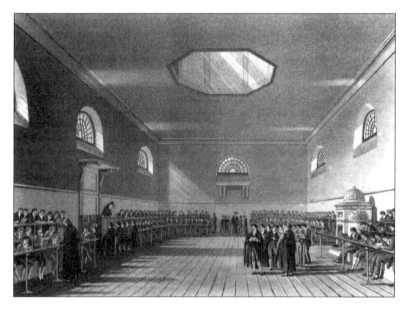

Ackermann print of the new Charterhouse schoolroom, viewed from the east end. This shows it with its original layout. Five boys are beneath the dais under scrutiny from the schoolmaster
(from Quick: Charterhouse: A History of the School)

In 1862, when Mrs. Turbutt of Ogston was enquiring about a Prep. School in Brighton for her two sons, the Headmaster's wife was more eager to impress her with good "connections" than with health and hygiene:

> Lady Mary Hoare's sons have both gone from our House to Eton
> & have been very satisfactorily placed. Our own eldest son is at
> Rugby & we have three pupils who go up next year – others are in
> preparation for Eton, Marlborough, Wellington College, etc. [In a
> later letter she added] Lady Ackland-Hood's son is with us. As the
> Honble. Mrs. F. Anson resides in your County I may mention that
> her son has been with us for the last year & a half.

Rather unfortunately, when the bill for the Turbutt boys' first term
came to Ogston Hall in April 1863 there was some dispute over
whether Richard should have been charged at 80 guineas, the same as
William, or at only 60 guineas, as he was less than nine years old.
Gladwin Turbutt, their father, pointed out rather acidly in a letter to
the Headmaster, "I believe it is not unusual in the case of Brothers to
make a reduction in the scale of charges". However, the small
misunderstanding was resolved, and the boys remained at No. 23,
Montpelier Crescent, Brighton, until they went on to Harrow.

Towards the end of the 19th century the position of Matron in
boarding schools had become well established, and mothers could
feel that there was, in effect, a mother substitute to look after their
children. Not all, perhaps, as thoroughly satisfied as the mother of
George Strutt may have been, to receive the following letter from
Mrs. Sanderson in May 1889. Mrs. Sanderson was the wife of the
Headmaster of George's Prep. School in Elstree, Hertfordshire. She
wrote on 8th May 1889, the day after George's arrival in Elstree:

> Yr. dear little son is very bright & says very decidedly indeed that
> he likes Elstree very much ... and 'the boys in his room'. <u>Yes, very</u>
> much – and that he has seen <u>no new ones</u> in his dormitory crying...
> I know this will comfort you. It is such a wrench to send one's
> children away... Mrs. Thayre, our boys' Nurse & Head Matron ...
> will carefully attend to all yr. instructions ... do write to <u>me</u>
> whenever & <u>as often</u> as you feel the least inclined to ask about
> anything. We will take the greatest care of him.

A week later a rather less effusive letter arrived from the Head
Matron, which may have raised a few doubts about her professional
qualifications, though not about her motherly qualities:

> Madam,
>
> I am very pleased to say Master Strutt is quite well and very

> happy... You may be quite sure I shall take every care of him   the Trowes fit very well but the other things have not come yet you shal have a post card as soon as they arrive   with duity believe me
>
> Yours respecfuly   e.Thayre

Not all boys were suited to a Public School education, even if the fees were affordable. Harold FitzHerbert was a pupil living with Rev. James Clark in Horncastle in 1876. He was being prepared for Wellington College, but his Aunt Judith was doubtful about sending him there, and Clark was also in two minds. He wrote to her in April:

> Among a great number ... I should say that ... instead of sharpening his wits, would bewilder them, and he would take refuge among the athletes. He is however not the kind of boy who would get on at a Public School, and as he has to earn his living, he must not go to a school merely to say that he has been there or to join in games.

In June Clark reported that he found it:

> ...impossible to do anything with him in the way of 'cram' and without that ... success in these days in competitive examination generally is hopeless".

So Harold's future remained a problem until a little 'influence' later resulted in a job with Barclay's Bank.

Letters Home

> I long to be stopping at the top of Ashburn hill to lock wheels or spinning along the Compton Street.

Alleyne FitzHerbert, at Charterhouse, December 1829.

About clothes

A child's first letter home was often about something vital, missing from his luggage. Frederic Arkwright wrote from school in Seagrave, in February 1816:

Dear Father,

... George has left a box at Rock House with all his books in and I believe you will find it under the stairs... I have not time to write any more now. [A frequent remark in letters from school.]

Clothes were often mislaid. Frederic complained in 1818, "My worst jacket was not packed up". William FitzHerbert, at Charterhouse with his brother Richard in 1819, wrote home, "I should like you to send with our stockings a night shirt or two, and night cap and ... two pairs of shoes as we can do with these things". In 1823 the plea was:

We think we must have some trowsers & waistcoats made, not jackets, as we have only got one pair of fustians apiece which will get very dirty... We also want if you please a few towels, as we have not got any.

In October 1824, Sir William Boothby, who was in London at the time, offered to take the boys out of school one Saturday for a treat. William wrote home:

...for which reason I wish to know if we may have a pair of trousers & waistcoat apiece now instead of at Christmas. We should not want coats but our trowsers that are our best now, having been washed last holidays have shrunk a good deal & are hardly good enough to go out in. We shall want a pair at Christmas if we do not have them now, & we will (if we have them now) take care to have them made large enough.

[Reader, you may need to read this letter more than once.]

Alleyne FitzHerbert, at Charterhouse in 1828, had trouble with stockings. Writing to his father, he asked:

Pray tell Mamma that the new stockings are a little too large for me but they say they will shrink with washing. They are very tearable too as I have made two holes already by simply pulling them on and as they are very large that was not very hard pulling to get them on.

The worst near mishap with clothes affected Anthony FitzHerbert, towards the end of the Summer Term at Harrow in 1834. On 3rd July he wrote:

My dear Papa,

I am writing in a great hurry to ask you to order a pair of cloth trowsers for me as soon as possible for those that I have been wearing have been mended so often that they wont mend any more, and are split smack up.

Six days later he wrote in some agitation, "My trousers are not come yet". But a postscript added before the letter was posted on the following day reads, "I got my black trowsers just in time, for they came the night <u>before</u> Speech Day, and they fit very well".

By 1866 when William Turbutt arrived at Harrow, 'School Uniform' rules had firmed up. William wrote anxiously to his mother: "Will you see that the trowsers before you send them have pockets made in front. Will you also send another flannel as I have lost the one which I have" [altered to 'had']. In June 1869 his brother Richard was asking, "Will you be able to send me a white waistcoat?" and William was "very much in want of a new tail coat as the one I wear is now quite worn out". Again in May 1872 he asked if he might "get an order for a white waistcoat as everybody wears them this quarter".

George Strutt at Elstree in May 1889 wrote home urgently: "It is so awffly hot now... My flannels have not come from Swears & Wells so please write to them about them". With relief he reported four days later: "My flannels have come". George also had trouble with things going missing during term time. A checklist made out by the Matron in 1891 recorded as follows:

2 prs shoes	– 1 pr missing
4 flannel shirts	– 1 missing
4 night shirts	– 1 missing
4 vests	– 1 missing
18 handkerchiefs	– 17 missing

No time to write

"I think that we should not have written quite so soon but I cannot withstand the pleasure of writing". So wrote William FitzHerbert just after his return to school in October 1819. But for some children writing home was a chore; schools unceasingly encouraged boarders to write regularly. Time was often set aside specifically for writing letters home.

John Lace, at Bromsgrove School in February 1846, wrote to his sister Fanny:

> I like this place pretty well; at least some things in it I like, but others are very disagreeable. You will wonder why I am writing this so well ... but the fact is, this is our writing time and ... we can write letters, only we write them like a copy.

This is written in very careful 'copperplate'. The rest of the letter is in ordinary handwriting, obviously written in free time, as he ends with, "As there is such a deafening noise here at present I can't write more".

A similar difficulty is mentioned in one of Richard FitzHerbert's letters to his sister Selina in 1819. "We are very sorry that we have blotted our letter in such a manner but the boys shake so that one can hardly write".

Crossings-out and corrections in a different hand are indications that a teacher or another adult had checked the letter. This was usual in schools for younger children. Compare the following letters from the young D'Ewes Coke, at Southwell, to his mother. The first was written in copperplate hand on double-ruled lines, and dated 3rd March 1814 when he was nearly ten years old.

> My dear Mamma
>
> I write to inform you that I and my brothers are very well, I hope you all are well at home. Edward goes on very well & is very happy at School. Give my love to Papa, Sisters & Brothers, & accept the same yourself. Mr. & Mrs. Footit present their respectful Compliments. I remain,
>
> my dear Mamma
>
> your affectionate Son
>
> D'Ewes Coke

The second letter was written on 15th 'August 1815. In spite of being over a year older, the excitement of his news, and perhaps the risk of being found out, clearly played havoc with his spelling and grammar:

> Dear Mamma
>
> I hope you are all very [well] at home, and we are the same hear…
> Theirs been a coach over … theirs a man tumpled down on his face
> and died on Sunday or Monday   a sergant broak is arlm, another
> brook they, and another his lef [leg?]   I saw them go past   I was
> in the gravel walk and we say we [he and his brother William] It
> wold be over before they got to Newark…

After signing the letter he realised that he would be in trouble when
his teacher read his mother's reply. The accident had happened early
on Saturday morning, and D'Ewes should not have been out on the
gravel path in front of the house to see the coach going through
Southwell at half past five. So he added a P.S.: "Don't writ any-thing
back about the [coach] or any or els Mrs. Footit will find out I got up
at half past five o'clock".

His mother appears to have kept quiet about it, but she also put the
letter away carefully to keep.

"Nothing to write about" or "No time" were frequent excuses made
by children at school. Frederic Arkwright wrote to his father from
Seagreave on 20th February and 6th March 1816, both short letters,
the first ending with "I have not time to write any more now" and the
second with "I have nothing ells to say now". In 1895 George Strutt
varied the formula by putting the excuse at the beginning of the letter:
"I am very sorry for not writing before this week but there has been
nothing to say". This, after a four week delay. Alleyne FitzHerbert,
writing to his father in 1830, apologised with his usual disarming
courtesy: "I have no more room which shows me that I am come to
the end of the proper allowance which is given to tire anyone's
patience with. So Good bye".

A letter which his brother William wrote in 1820 is entirely taken up
with reasons for not having time to write!

> Dear Father,
>
> I am sorry that I have not had time to write to you before but the
> whole of my [time] is spent in playing at football. For you must
> [know] that we get up in the morning at a quarter before seven and
> stay in till half past eight   the[n] we have only another hour to eat
> breakfast and I have to get another boy his breakfast and toast it.
> Then we stay in till twelve   then we eat dinner at one and are

from Tom Brown's Schooldays, illustrated by H.M. Brock

generally in till half after two   at half past two we have to go in to scool   then we stop in till half past four   then the gass is not lit and it is to dark to write now I think I have stated enough reasons why I did not write before but I have found a little bit of time today   but you see by the writing I was in a great hurry   our places are taken for Monday the eleventh in the Manchester Mail ...

I remain your aff. Son

W FitzHerbert

However, convincing this is, the most unanswerable instance of having 'Nothing to say' is provided by Anthony, at Harrow with his younger brother John in 1834. John had written a page with a few bits of news and a report on how bad the weather had been, and concluded with "I have nothing more to say, only I think Anthony is going to write, So Goodbye   Ever your Affte. Son   John FitzHerbert".

There is more than a page of the writing paper left. It is blank.

Home Thoughts

Longing for home and holidays is a regular feature of letters from school, both gratifying and painful for parents. William FitzHerbert, describing his and Richard's daily routine at Charterhouse in July 1819, wrote: "We get up about quarter pas five wash and brush our hair   We go out and think how we shall spend the Holidays". In December 1821 they still looked forward to holidays, but seem to have been lighter in spirit. "Fine fun going down   we shall get some pea shooters and shoot Jimmy if he comes near us ... hope we shall have jolly holidays". And the following year in December Richard anticipated "some fine fun next holidays reading plays over the fireplace".

On 5th October 1824 William wrote to his father, "I and Alleyne take a walk together every morning ... with us it was a fine day & we thought of you travelling up the hills". This was a thought probably prompted by Alleyne, who was very attached to his home and his home county, and who frequently counted the days to holiday time. In October 1825 he wrote "...only eleven days to the holidays". In July 1826 it was "...only three weeks on Wednesday ... it will soon come. And I shall be very cozy". In November 1827 he wrote to Anthony: "It was only 4 weeks yesterday to the Holidays and then Hurra for old Tissington again".

In a note to his sister Maria in October 1829 Alleyne wrote: "I suppose you have found plenty of fine fun at Tissington since you have been away such a long time without seeing the dear old place". Later that year, in December, he expressed his feelings at length in a letter to his father:

> I long to be stopping at the top of Ashburne hill to lock wheels or spinning along the Compton Street ... I must ask William Johnson to teach me ... that I may be able to fly-fish a little in the May holidays for the Dear little Trout in the Dear little Dove. I want very much to go to Beresford to see Cotton's fishing house... I mean to take long walks to all points of the compass from Tissington as I hardly know more of Derbyshire than I do of Kent.

Some years later, in his first year at Cambridge, on 8th May 1834, Alleyne remarked in a letter home, "Today is the great day at Tissington and I hope the Hall Well may do best". He went on to say how pretty Cambridge looked in the Spring, but concluded that "the country can never be anything but flat, and so as a Derbyshire man I must contend for its being ugly".

Next to holidays the best thing for Derbyshire children away at school was to find some other Derbyshire fellows or some trace of an older acquaintance. Richard Arkwright tried to justify his taking part in unauthorised boating at Eton in 1798 by assuring his father that "One of the Cavendishes steers in one of the boats".

Frederic Arkwright, newly arrived at Eton in September 1818, seems to have felt quite at home. He told his mother:

> I have found one of Edward's old schoolfellows ... he says Mr. Heptinstall used to cob Edward with a ruler a great deal. I met a gentleman yesterday ... he said he remembered Arkwrights major, minor, and minimus. I have found Uncle Charles' name down in the school-room. There is a boy here of the name of Sted   he lives near Chesterfield, he knows the Gells of Hopton... I have not found the Mundys and Curzons yet.

The FitzHerbert boys found a few members of other Derbyshire families at school during the 1820s and 1830s. In September 1821

Richard told his mother, "...there are about 40 new boys there are the two Wilmots ... the Wilmots have fine agricultural countenances". In November 1829 Alleyne wrote home, "Jessop will come down by the Mail this time with me as far as Derby which will be very comfortable as I shall have a companion to speak to". Anthony remarked in 1833: "...we had never seen Meynell before, he is in our House...".

A letter from Richard Turbutt to his mother in June 1863 epitomises the feelings of all eight-year-olds at Prep. School: "I often dream that I have gone home for the holidays. I often think of going home. Howe glad we shall be when the 31st of July comes". But he also discovered some Derbyshire fellows. In June 1866 he mentioned, "Both the Cavendishes came back this term but the eldest is going to leave for the navy at the end of it".

William Turbutt established another sort of link with his home county in 1871, one not so easily available for earlier generations. "Thanks very much for the County papers which I have been reading", he wrote. "I like seeing them very much".

Schoolwork

> I think I shall like Howson, my new Form Master, very much so far, but I believe he can make himself very objectionable when he chooses.

– George Strutt at Harrow, 1895.

The daily timetable

Hours spent in class were long, and lessons also had to be prepared for the next day. Apart from supervised 'Prep.', keen scholars studied in their spare time, often getting up very early to do so. In the early 19th century it was also quite usual to have some formal lessons before breakfast.

At a private Girls' School in Southwell in 1814, Elizabeth Coke told her mother, "We get up early in the morning and say our lessons before breakfast". When they started at Charterhouse in 1820, William and Richard FitzHerbert had an hour in class before breakfast at 8.30. Then they had two and a half hours of lessons before dinner at midday, and the same in the afternoon. In 1823 William mentioned, "We have begun Virgil again. We do about ten hours a day". [But perhaps it just felt like that.]

In March 1847 John Lace at Bromsgrove told his sister:

> I am beginning now to work in earnest. On whole school days I am occupied all the day except from 12 to half past one & then I have often to copy notes &c.

The day at Repton in the 1860s began with prayers at 7.15, then lessons until 8.45. There was half an hour of supervised preparation from 10.00 to 10.30, followed by two hours of lessons. Afternoon school was from 3.00 to 5.30. At Harrow in 1892 George Strutt reported, "We have about nine hours and a half work every day".

At Abbotsholme, the 'New School', much less time was spent on formal lessons. The 1891 Timetable specified that the boys got up at 6.10, had military drill, physical exercises or a run at 6.30, followed by First School from 6.45 to 7.30. After a ten minute religious service there was breakfast. However, it was noted that "every boy will have a light meal immediately after rising", which prompted the reporter from the Pall Mall Gazette to exclaim, "Oh! that one had been born in the days of The New School, instead of in those of the Old!"

Breakfast at 7.40 was followed by Dormitory Parade, bed-making and teeth-cleaning, and Second School began at 8.30, during the first period of which (8.30-9.15) "the boys visit, in batches under captains, the earth cabinets in the garden". At 10.45 there was lunch until 11.15, "and, if fine, Lung Drill in the open air, stripped to the waist". Third School followed, and Dinner at one o'clock.

The afternoon was taken up with games, gardening and other organised activities such as play-readings or rehearsals, music and singing. Supper was at 8.30, followed by Chapel, and then Lights Out at 9.00.

School Subjects

Children in wealthy families were generally taught reading, writing and simple arithmetic at home by a parent, older sibling or governess. For many girls that was the total of their education. Almost all the time at Public School was spent on Latin and Greek. The few Grammar Schools that existed were in fact prohibited by ancient law from teaching any other subjects. What we would now regard as essentials – mathematics, modern languages, history, geography, the sciences – all these came into schools as 'extras' which had to be paid for separately.

Most of the work the FitzHerberts had to do at Charterhouse involved translating Latin and Greek Classics into English, but they also had to memorise long passages, word for word. In 1824 William wrote, "I am learning Cicero now instead of Homer" and "We are reading the Georgics of Virgil which I think amusing". His brother Alleyne's opinion of the Georgics was "very easy except the names of the plants and tools for cultivation which are very hard to remember as I do not know what kind of things they are". This illustrates the kind of 'learning by rote' which was typical of education at the time.

Alleyne also complained that the master "set such long lessons, about 25 lines to learn by heart, that we could never repeat a word of it". One way of memorising was described by Alleyne in a letter of 1829: "I know 21 Odes of Horace, and 2 fellows in our room last night in bed capped verses together with me and we went on a long time".

One of the very few references to subjects other than the Classics is in a letter from Alleyne in 1829: "Russell begins to attend much more than he used to about Arithmetic which I am very glad of, for I like it very much". Another reference is made in 1830, when Alleyne mentioned that, after repeating "about fifty lines of Homer by heart ... and three chapters of De Senectute of Cicero", he had "half an Hour ... with Dicken who teaches us Algebra &c".

The FitzHerbert boys found, as some children still do, that subjects which were not taught in school were more interesting, and studied them on their own. William wrote to his father in November 1824, "I shall study the little book Mama gave me & I think by the Holidays I shall know a good deal of Geography". The fact that Sir Henry was then on his way to Barbados must have contributed to this zeal for geography.

In February 1825 Lady Agnes wrote to her husband, "The Boys have got a rage to learn French at the Charter House, not with a Master but amongst themselves and they have taken Grammars &

Dictionaries and Alleyne is to correct excercises". (It would appear that Alleyne had already learnt some French at home, perhaps from Selina).

In 1829 Alleyne mentioned to his father that he was teaching himself Italian. "Lately I have not got on so much in Italian as I did at first, as I am now rather in want of an explainer and teacher, but Selina will soon get me on again". And he went on, "Last Saturday I took a volume of Gil Blas from Henrietta Street [their London house] and I have been reading it this week to keep up my French a bit".

In May 1820 Frederic Arkwright, at Eton, mentioned, "I believe I am to begin Euclid soon with Mr. Hexter". Mr. Hexter was a tutor working in the school, but not a regular member of the staff. This was a common arrangement; and what D'Ewes Coke (senior) had in mind in February 1820 when he made a special trip to Shrewsbury. His Diary records that he wanted to speak to Dr. Butler, the Head, "on D'Ewes' general attainment & industry & on the practicality of his having French next half year". (Unfortunately he never found an opportune moment, either at or after dinner).

Gradually Greek began to drop out of the normal curriculum and French or another modern language came in. Frank Arkwright, at Heath Vicarage in October 1852, told his Grandmama, "I am learning the Latin declensions and verbs... I learn also the French verbs and write a French exercise". The following month he wrote thanking her for:

> ...the pretty little Globe. I understand the Meridians and Parallels, we have a lesson in Geography every day... I have a history of England... We have learnt our Positions in Dancing and can jump and cross our feet.

The Turbutt boys at Brighton in 1863, preparing for Harrow, had a relatively 'modern' curriculum. Their weekly timetable as shown on a Weekly Report Form was as follows:

Sun.	Scripture History Poetry			
Mon.	Writing Arithmetic Poetry Latin Grammar Prose Composition			
Tue.	Geography History Writing Latin Grammar Latin Translation			
Wed.	History French			

Thur. Geography   Writing   Latin Grammar
Latin Translation   Prose Composition
Fri. History   Dictation   Arithmetic   Latin Grammar
Latin Translation   Prose Composition
Sat. Geography   Arithmetic   Poetry   Latin Grammar
Prose Composition   French

There was still great emphasis on learning passages of prose or poetry and repeating it, word for word. Richard Turbutt made this clear in a letter to his father: "On Sunday we had repetition of all the hymns we have learnt in the term ... next Sunday we are going to have the repetition of the Scripture".

The Turbutts' timetable at Brighton in 1863 suggests a curriculum similar to what Harold FitzHerbert had to face in the Entrance Examination for Wellington College in 1876.

1. Dictation with efficiency in Writing & Spelling.
2. Arithmetic. Fractions and (instead of Greek or German) Decimals, and 1st Book of Euclid to Prop.20 [Geometry].
3. French. Grammar to end of Regular Conjugations – construing a French Fable or easy passage in prose.
4. Latin Grammar. Accidence and Translation of easy sentences in Caesar, and easy exercises.

There were also questions to answer on Bible History, English History and Geography.

It is worth noticing that Greek, though not compulsory, is still an option. It had still not disappeared in 1889 when George Strutt wrote from his Prep. School: "It is so nice in the ninth Form. We have begun Greek". (This is remarkable! In his letters he still wrote 'pencil' as 'pencle' and spelt his sister Isabel's name 'Isable').

Lessons for Girls

In the 18th century and for most of the 19th century the education of girls had little in common with schooling for boys. In a few rare cases a daughter might be introduced to Latin by a well-educated parent, as Selina FitzHerbert was, by Sir Henry. In a letter to him on 27th September 1820, having given various bits of family news, she wrote, "Hic concludam epistolam meam, fatigatus eris (I hope you will understand my Latin)". And with some more information added to

33

the letter the next day, she wrote, "I popt in that bit of Latin to show you that I have not quite forgot it". At this time she was just two months short of her twelfth birthday.

Most girls' education, however, followed the lines suggested by Erasmus Darwin of Derby, in his book "A Plan for Female Education", published in 1797. His view was that girls'minds would be damaged by too much learning, and his recipe consisted of a great deal of general knowledge of a superficial kind.

> Great eminence in almost anything is sometimes injurious to a young lady ... great strength of character ... is liable to alarm both her own and the other sex. [For this reason] young ladies should play, sing and dance only so well as to amuse themselves and their friends. [Geography and History might be taught, but Natural History would be] easier to their comprehensions and thence more interesting and agreeable to them. [For this, he recommended] Mr. Bewick's account of quadrupeds with wood-prints.

Taste, drawing and embroidery were important, and Heathen Mythology was necessary to appreciate paintings and statues, but he warned that "as a great part of this mythology consists of personify'd vices, much care should be taken". Girls might also learn about contemporary crafts and manufactories such as the "cotton works on the river Derwent in Derbyshire" or potteries and ironworks. It would be an advantage to young ladies, he thought, to know of such developments "as they are in future life to become companions".

Some girls' schools aimed at Dr. Darwin's ideals without quite living up to them. Elizabeth Bradshaw of Holbrook attended "a school kept by 2 Miss Stubbs at Wirksworth" in 1805, when she was seven years old. The work, she remembered, consisted of "the use of the Globes, the names of the Gods & Godesses, and embroidery with a little drawing". At the age of about sixteen she was at a school for young ladies in Doncaster, where there was a French teacher and also:

> Masters of every description ... Drill and dancing masters, Piano, Harp & Guitar, Drawing and Writing and Flower painting, each separate.

Some of the girls' fathers were army officers serving in India whose wives had joined them, and Elizabeth remarked how the girls tried everything, but "failed in each of course, taking little back but long bills".

Another Derbyshire girl, Harriett Wager of Longstone, was in school at Bubnell Hall in March 1862. She wrote to her brother Albert:

> I think I am getting on very well in my Music, writing, spelling, arithmetic and reading but I must leave you to judge as self-praise is no reccomendation [sic] I am doing a beautiful piece of work [embroidery] the subject is "King Charles the First taking leave of his children [before his execution]. I was reading about the same yesterday and I quite enjoyed it.

A few years earlier she had been at school in Bakewell and wrote a number of 'letters' to her brothers and sisters. Whether they were actually sent as real letters we do not know. Those that survive are actually written in school exercise books.

One, dated 30th September 1859, begins: "I have the greatest pleasure in writing a weekly letter to you, the hope of an answer always increases the gratification". It then goes on: "I will tell you about Sponge. It is a marine production..." And three pages follow, describing the nature of sponges and their uses. Another, to "My dear Hannah", begins "hoping you will answer me very soon", but continues, "I will endeavour to describe this week's Bible lessons" and launches into the story of Joseph and his brothers.

In an actual letter to her cousin Matilda in 1860, when Harriett was at Church View, Bakewell, Harriett mentioned "our catechism of British Biography" – questions and answers to be learnt off by heart about famous people. Some of her letters from Bubnell Hall convey the piecemeal nature of her schooling. As a Geographical Exercise she had to copy out the following and other similar questions and answers:

> Mention the capitals of France; Spain; Portugal; and Switzerland.
> Of France, Paris; Spain, Madrid; Portugal, Lisbon; Switzerland, Berne.
> How many counties does England contain? Forty.

Historical Exercises included the following [not even in order of time]:

> How long did John reign?

Where did Hengist and Horsa land?
Who did Cromwell defeat at Worcester?

"Orthographical Exercises" (it sounds more important than 'spelling') which Harriett also had to copy, were supposed to teach the difference between 'beer' and 'bier'; 'reed' and 'read'; 'sent', 'scent' and 'cent', and many others.

Harriett's copy-books had the headline written by Miss Wilkinson, of Bridge House, Bakewell, and Harriett had to copy it on every line down the page of the book. The writing gave scraps of disconnected information of the kind which was then considered suitable (as in Dr. Darwin's opinion) for the female mind:

The Burning of Moscow. Sept. 14, 1839.
Dundee, a Town in the East of Scotland.
Avignon, a City in the South of France.

In this latter case Harriett's writing was somewhat larger than the teacher's headline, so that the last three lines of her writing end with 'Fra', then 'F' and finally 'of'.

By the end of the 19th century some Public Schools had put Modern Languages on the curriculum, as at Repton, where Natural Science was also taught, as well as Drawing and Singing. In 1887 the opening of the Engineering Workshop caused some concern among traditionalists. Other Derbyshire schools, such as Chesterfield Grammar School, were also at this time putting more emphasis on Maths, French, German and Science, and less on Latin.

St. Elphin's School for Girls, which was re-sited in Darley Dale in 1904, emphasised religious subjects because of its historic connection with the Church of England. The Religious Curriculum included Holy Scripture, Daily and Occasional Services, The Catechism, Church History and the Articles of Religion. The general Curriculum offered History, Geography, Arithmetic, French and Latin; and also Music, Drawing and Callisthenics. Cookery was timetabled for Saturdays, being regarded as a pastime rather than a proper school subject.

Rewards and Punishments

Pupils were encouraged to work hard by a system of weekly

promotions and demotions in class or from one class to another. A boy might also have to stay in when others were at play, to re-learn a lesson or to do extra work; the cane was always available for more serious sins of omission or commission. At first there were no formal Termly reports, but the Head or a Housemaster might write a complaint to a parent at any time, and the pupil would have to think of a good excuse for his idleness or misbehaviour. Towards the end of the 19th century the cane was less widely used, and schools began to issue regular reports. The awarding of prizes, usually books, for good work or good conduct was also a late 19th century introduction.

The Arkwright boys at Eton in 1798 were quite blasé about corporal punishment. They wanted to take part in unauthorised rowing, which would mean missing roll call. Richard wrote to tell his father, "We shall be flogged about twice a week but that is quite a trifle". Richard FitzHerbert, new to Charterhouse in October 1819, thought it newsworthy to tell his father, "One of the boys who had done something wrong was just going to be flogged and Mr. Russell had sent for the rod but however, he excused him". Two years later he reported, "4 boys are to be flogged for not doing their Holidays task, lucky we did ours".

In April 1817, D'Ewes Coke noted in his Diary a complaint he made to Mr. Bidon, the Headmaster of Risley Grammar School, where his sons, D'Ewes, William and Edward were boarding:

> I requested he would discontinue cuffing them on account of the danger of causing deafness by an intemperate blow on the head & that he wou'd substitute a Strap or Rod for the hands instead.

His remonstrance had no effect, however, and on 20th July he again

> Wrote to Mr. Bidon on the subject of cuffing boys as a punishment & apprized him of my intention to remove William if it was not discontinued.

Whether the cuffing ended or not, William was unhappy at Risley. His father's Diary entry for 3rd November 1817 reads:

> In the Evening had the unpleasant intelligence that William had ran away from Risley to Nottingham & had persuaded a less Boy

than himself to go with him, others having refused. Wrote to Mr. Bidon to desire he would flog him most severely before the whole school.

Even without a flogging, a bad report from school to an unsympathetic father put a boy in an unenviable position. D'Ewes Coke's Diary for Sunday, 18th June 1820 mentions his eldest son, D'Ewes, then at Shrewsbury, who had come home with a sealed letter from his Headmaster:

> Dr. Butler, in his letter with D'Ewes, complains of his having been more inattentive this last half year than before & advises that he should be worked in French Grammar, Syntax, Cicero, Virgil & Xenophon, every day during the holiday, to check the habit of indolence... It was almost impossible to have a more unpleasant account of a Boy of 16, already very backward compared with what I was at the same age, & I spoke to him very severely on the subject.

John Lace, newly settled at Bromsgrove in February 1846, wrote at some length to his sister on the subject of punishments:

> I am in the IV Form under Mr. Eaton & he is very strict... I am rather afraid I shall be put down into the III Form as I can hardly do the work we have... There are some fellows in the V Form much less [younger] than I am while ... there are older fellows in the III.

A month later he was more cheerful:

> I have had only three impositions & the whole Form had them, six have been caned, & many a hundred lines have been written by some. Some fellows seem never to learn their lessons & then they are sure to have a hundred lines of Virgil to write out or else a caning. I hope I shall escape the caning, for they are rather awful   he makes a blood-mark every cut. Sometimes I think he is rather too severe.

John did not refer to caning again so he must have escaped. In October 1846 he wrote:

> I feel very jolly at present. The Quarter's marks were given out yesterday & I gained four places... I was head in mathematics... I was not nearly as high in Classics and Divinity.

Promotions and demotions are often mentioned when Derbyshire children were writing to their parents, the former more often than the latter. Perhaps Derbyshire children were just brighter and more hard-working than others? In 1829 Alleyne FitzHerbert told his aunt, "Today I was put up a form for my holiday task with I did last Holydays", adding honestly, "with a good deal of help from Selina though".

In 1863 the two little Turbutts wrote home to say, "We have both got prizes for holiday task which we did not expect", Richard adding that his prize was "a nice poetry book". William, however, had to explain about his Weekly Report. "The Reason why I have not got good marks is that I used improper words" – which is open to more than one interpretation! Subsequently he wrote to Mama, "I told Papa why I lost my marks on Sunday. Those that I lost in the week were because I talked in schooltime. Mrs. Cook says that if I lose them this week I shall lose my play".

More trouble for the Turbutt boys is indicated by a bill, due to be paid to Thomas Anscombe "For work done at 22 Montpelier Crescent" dated 21st June 1864:

> ...to Paperhanger repairing paper behind the door in Schoolroom consequent upon having been daubed with ink, including paper for ditto 2s. 6d.

Whether one or both boys were guilty, or what the punishment was, apart from Papa getting the Bill, is not recorded.

George Strutt, a very new boy at Elstree on 17th May 1889 wrote to ask his mother, "Please tell Iisabel [his sister, mis-spelt] I am nearly top of my class". A fortnight later he reported, "I am top of the tenth still". Early in June, "I have got my remove to the ninth". In September he wrote, "I have got my remove to the eighth form in arithmetic". [The 10th Form was the lowest and the 1st Form the highest class, as in most schools then; and pupils were often in different Forms for different subjects]. By October 1890 he could claim "I think I will be pretty high this week in the seventh form... I came out very low last week" and he enclosed the Form Order showing him 8th out of 11. In March 1891 he had to admit, "I was only fifth in form last week but I will be pretty high next". And in his next letter was a copy of the official

23 Montpelier Crescent
Brighton.

May 23rd
1863.

My dear Mama,
I hope you
are quite well.
I thank you for
your nice letter, and
the seeds which you
sent me.
On Friday we were

drilled after tea
Will you tell me how
my garden is looking.
I was very good at my
drawing lesson yester-
day.
With love from,
Your affec'te son
Richard

Richard Turbutt writing from Prep. School in 1863

List with Strutt at the top with 1143 marks, and the lowest boy with only 685.

When he went on to Harrow George found the competition tougher. In May 1893 he wrote, "I was low in form this week, I can't make out why, because I am working as hard as possible". In November 1895 he was again having to explain:

> I am verry sorry for getting such a wretched report & coming out so low in Form... [This] was not due to neglect of work as you seem to think ... never got a single punishment of any kind ... chiefly due to some bad prose I did... should be really high next fortnight.

Assessment of teachers

Promotions and punishments depended a good deal, of course, on the character of individual teachers. Children's response to, and views on, particular teachers varied as much then as now. John Lace, who thought Mr. Eaton at Bromsgrove might be "rather too severe", had been very impressed a few years earlier with a teacher at his Prep. School in Easingwold:

> Mr. Carnac has taught George and myself to jump with poles. Mr. Carnac can easily jump over a hedge above a yard high. I can jump over a pole about two feet high. He has also showed us how to drop from high branches of trees.

George Strutt at Harrow, being a good deal older, was rather more critical. In February 1893 he complained, "Mr. Stephen is beastly this term & has not been married yet". With relief he reported in May, "Mr. Stephen is far nicer this Term. He has got a very nice little house ready for Miss Weldon".

In October he mentioned to his mother, "I am in Mr. Owen's Form... he is a very slack sort of chap". In his next letter he told her, "I get on all right with Owen, he seems a very weak-minded sort of man though very good tempered". George's opinion of the Upper Sixth Form Master was that he "has no more idea of keeping order than a fly". And to support this view he told how "The other day a chap let a lot of mice loose in the form room, & he did not even take the trouble of finding out who it was". In 1895 George summed up another teacher in the classic comment:

> I think I shall like Howson, my new Form Master, very much so far, but I believe he can make himself very objectionable when he chooses.

Free Time

> It will not exceed 7 Guineas each... We flatter ourselves you will pay for us, as you have often told us you do not mind expence when it is not improperly applied.

- Richard Arkwright at Eton with his two brothers in 1798, asking Father to pay their boating expenses.

Games and Pastimes

In the 18th and early 19th century, when not actually in class or doing supervised preparation, boys were left to occupy their time more or less as they wished. Occasionally a teacher might organise cricket or some other activity, but formal school games were established only gradually in the second half of the 19th century.

S. A. Pears, Headmaster of Repton, 1854–1874, saw it as a positive feature of his school that the boys were unsupervised for three or four hours a day, believing that they should learn how to occupy their free time for themselves. He did, however, give them the opportunity to play Cricket, Rugby and Fives, and to go swimming in the Trent, if they wished, and allowed matches between Houses and against other schools. Under a later Head a Photographic Club was formed.

In contrast, the "New School", Abbotsholme, included in its 1894 Prospectus a wide range of activities and team games, which were "compulsory for all, to obviate loafing &c". These included bee-keeping, gardening and farming, which prompted a reporter from the Pall Mall Gazette to remark:

> The captains of our Elevens generally leave school on terms of perfect familiarity with twenty-two yards of cricket-pitch... At Abbotsholme they will mark out the year by seedtime and

harvest … as much as by the date when cricket begins and football ends.

Boredom was certainly a feature of early boarding school life. When William Perrin visited his nephew Anthony FitzHerbert at Winchester in April 1794 they went for a walk "which on most half Holidays they take once & Whole Holidays twice in fine weather & good Exercise it is". Good exercise indeed, but after a few times, terribly boring.

In July 1819, William FitzHerbert at Charterhouse wrote to his sister Selina:

> We now get up very early   we play at horses a great deal in the green. Mr. Young plays at cricket evry Wednesday and Saturday with the boys.

The next term he and Richard mentioned hockey, hoops and horses, football and hide-and-seek, and wrote about "a very good bonfire on the fifth of November and plenty of fireworks". Two years later Alleyne reported having the same games, with the addition of "fly the garter, which is nearly the same as leapfrog".

In March 1828 Alleyne mentioned what he clearly considered a great improvement on Hoops:

> We have a little four-wheeled carriage here now and we pull it round the Green and have a ride in it in turns, and gives us plenty of exercise as we go round as fast as we can.

The main emphasis here is on simple "exercise" as it was for Anthony FitzHerbert's walks in 1794, but when John FitzHerbert went to Harrow in September 1834 he found that Hockey, Football and Rackets were played, as well as House cricket and inter-school cricket. In 1836 he mentioned matches against Eton and Winchester.

In winter, snow and ice provided a welcome if rather brief change of games. At the end of November 1827 Alleyne wrote to his mother from Charterhouse:

> There have been two or three days of snow … and we have made slides on the stones on the Fives Courts and they were pretty good slides.

Again, in February 1828:

> This morning the playground was iced all over. We had some

pretty good slides on it … we have had some snow balling matches.

Ten years later, John reported from Harrow on 20th January:

We have some very good skating on Steel's pond, where Wordsworth often comes, he is a very good skater indeed.

The Arkwright Boys

Richard Arkwright and his brothers Robert and Peter were at Eton in February 1798, and a short series of Richard's letters help to illustrate how sports developed in Public Schools in the face of bland indifference or active opposition from masters; and how little supervision there was of the boys' free time. The first letter which mentions rowing is dated 5th March. Richard gets straight to the point:

Dear Father,

My Brothers and myself think of pulling in a six-oared boat after Easter, and if you will give us leave and money we shall be very happy… The expence attending it will be but trifling to you.

It will not exceed 7 Guineas each. The parents of all the other boys pay the expence; …We flatter ourselves you will pay for us, as you have often told us you do not mind expence when it is not improperly applied… Pray write soon on account of ordering a boat from London.

I am in haste

Your dutiful son

Richard Arkwright

We must assume that his father did not instantly agree, in spite of the gentle arm-twisting, because the next letter, on 14th March, begins:

I am afraid you do not rightly understand about the boat. It is a custom … between Easter and midsummer to pull in boats. …the Queen came to see it last year and intends to come this. One of the Cavendishes steers in one of the boats. One of Dr. Heath's [the Headmaster] own sons steers.

If further proof was needed that boating was a reasonable and innocuous pastime, Richard reported that some of the Masters watched the boys rowing and made no attempt to stop them.

About four months later a long letter from Richard told a complicated tale of the boys going to Maidenhead in defiance of threats of being expelled, uproar among boys and Masters, with Richard's private Tutor being accused of calling the oarsmen "a parcel of blackguards" and the Headmaster himself being taken ill.

A letter to the boys' father in December 1801 from Dr. Goodall, the newly-appointed Head, laid no blame on the Arkwright boys, but stated that in future absence from roll-call by "parties in the boats" would be regarded as "a very flagrant offence".

A further letter from Dr. Goodall referred to the debts which the boys had run up. "Without knowing anything of their Water Expences", he wrote, "I have already expressed my apprehensions". And he suggested that their father should not pay their debts, as they had "richly deserved ... the personal inconveniences they may suffer from being dunned".

Another rather disturbing letter arrived at Willersley about the same time from the boys' Housemaster explaining about "the drinking of Porter in my House. I had suspicions that some of my family [the boys in his House] were in the habit of going to the Inn for it", but thought it had stopped. "So relaxed has the discipline been of late, that all errors have increased most generally", but he hoped that by "the present change of Master ... benefits will ensue". Dr. Goodall himself assured Richard Arkwright that he would do his best "to prevent a renewal of the Licence of the Tapster" and further explained that "In regard to the guns etc., I am shocked to find that such Irregularity has been systematically practised".

By 1820 when Frederic Arkwright, Peter's son, was at Eton the life of the school was rather more as one would expect. He mentioned three advantages of the school's situation on the river, near Windsor. The boys were allowed to go to the Castle, where Frederic saw the King "very plain" and where he also could benefit from the military presence:

> I went up to the riding school at the Horse Guards barracks in Windsor, on Saturday, and am going again to-morrow, it is 3s.6d a time, they teach you to ride and leap, and halt &c. [He also wanted

permission to go bathing]. All the boys bathe, and if you don't bathe of your own accord, the 5th Form fag you to do it, and to learn to swim, I am sure I don't think it would do me any harm, John Gell bathed the other day, I believe.

Outings and Treats

Charterhouse in the 1820s had no open country or river, but there were compensations when an outing was in prospect. The FitzHerbert boys had their grand-uncle, Lord St. Helens, and an aunt, Fanny FitzHerbert, both living in London; their father, Sir Henry, had a house there for some years. There were other Derbyshire friends who took them out of school for a treat when they were up in town. On Saturday, 22nd July 1826 Lord St. Helens scribbled a note to Sir Henry:

> I have just had the pleasure of a visit from Richard and Alleyne. Both in High health and joyous expectation of their promised good dinner at Mr. Arkwright's and succeeding treat to one of the minor Theatres. But whether to Astleys or Sadlers Wells they neither know nor care.

In March 1828 Alleyne, recently recovered from chicken pox, wrote to tell his father:

> I go out to Aunt Fanny every Saturday and Sunday... The Sunday before last Lord St. Helens took Aunt Fanny and myself in his carriage to the Zoological Gardens in the Regent's Park ... as he is a member of the Society. Amongst the animals we saw a Lynx which growled in a very odd manner. We saw some very nice Lapland Dogs there also.

Alleyne's younger brothers, Anthony and John, had an equally enjoyable Zoological outing in Bakewell in October 1831. They were then boarding at the Vicarage with Mr. Hodgson. Anthony wrote:

> There was a wild beast show here last week   Lions and tigers and loopard and all those sort of things. There were two very little monkeys there, not above six inches long... There was a great baboon with a very red nose that drank strong ale and an ourang-outang but that was a separate show and 2 shillings to see it. The Elephant drank things out of a bottle. I think it was the same that we saw at a play in London.

Minor Pastimes

For young children at a small private school in a Vicarage there were, of course, no opportunities for team games, but they might have hobbies of a fairly active kind. John W. Lace at Rev. S. J. Allen's in Easingwold had "three schoolfellows and five playfellows ... a girl called Mary Alice about eleven ... George about nine ... Elisabeth about eight". As activities the children did some gardening, kept rabbits and hens, and a good deal of time was taken up with the church. John told his sister in a letter of 10th August 1841:

> On Sunday there are three services   the first and second are like what you have and in the evening prayer and a sermon. On Wednesday there are the evening prayers and a sermon and on Fridays in the morning the morning prayers as far as the end of the Litany...

Outings tended to have an ecclesiastical flavour. In September John reported:

> We went to York the other [day] to see a Horticultural show... As we went early we were in time for the Minster service. There were eight little choristers in white gowns who sang very sweetly.

He was not allowed out on 5th November, to the bonfire, as he had been ill, but:

> I saw them out of the window. I think there were half a dozen rockets, some Roman candles, fancy fireworks, a jack in a box & plenty of squibs & crackers. I have got a Roman candle and a couple of pin-wheels which I bought of a man who came about with fireworks. I shall set them off when I am well.

Five years later, at Bromsgrove School, he found his leisure time less interesting than at Easingwold. In February he wrote, echoing many boys at boarding school, "This is a very dull part of the year as there are very few games". In October he told his sister, glumly, "We had half a holiday on Monday to have a game at foot-ball & we had another on Tuesday ... it is not at all a favourite game here ... Hoccy [sic] is all the go at present".

One novel pastime in the mid-nineteenth century was photography, provided there was an enthusiast on the Staff. James FitzHerbert took this up in 1859, and wrote to tell his Grandmama, Lady Agnes:

> I have been learning photographing here [at Shrewsbury] and can
> now take them pretty well but I made a good many bad mistakes at
> first and stained my hands a good deal with the chemicals. I think
> it will be so nice to be able to take photographs of all my friends
> and of buildings and landscapes... I shall be glad when I get a
> machine of my own and can photograph Mama and the baby
> without turning my fingers yellow.

The Turbutt boys at Prep. School in Brighton in the 1860s had more
organised games and activities, but even then, if all else failed, walks.
In his first term away from home, April 1863, Richard wrote to his
mother, "We went yesterday to the criket feild but we did not play
because we do not know it". William wrote a few days later, "We
went yesterday to the cricket field and had a nice game and in the
afternoon we took a walk on the Dyke road". In May Richard told
his Papa, "We have spent all our play hours in the cricket field or in
taking nice walks". In October he wrote, "We do not play cricket any
longer but we play at foot-ball it is great fun". But he added, of
course, "When it has been raining we go out for a walk".

They were also encouraged to have hobbies. "We are busy making
bookmarkers. I bought today a nice paintbox for nine pence which I
like very much", wrote William. Each boy had a patch of garden to
tend, and occasionally there was an evening talk or entertainment. In
March 1863:

> We had last Wensday [altered to Wednesday] a lecture on eclipses
> and tides and next time we are going to have one on spiders which
> I think will be very amusing.

In May, "There is a person coming to read one of Shakespeare's plays
this evening". In October Richard wrote telling his mother about a
visiting chemistry lecturer, who had

> A small balloon which he filled with gas   he held it with a string
> and gave it to some of the boys and it went up to the ceiling...
> afterwards we had an electric shock.

The Turbutt boys also had riding lessons from W. Wright, Whitehall
Yard, King's Road, at four shillings per hour, and went to Brills'
Royal Baths for swimming. But the most exciting day was at the end
of June 1863. Both boys wrote about it:

> We had a pic-nic at Bramber yesterday. We went in coaches by

the Shireham road. We went round the moat of the old castle there. We played at croquet while the others played at cricket. In the evening we had tea at the inn. We cheered as we came home.

In July they went to Bramber again and had "a few games at hare and hounds" and "tea out on the grass the same as dinner".

At Harrow excitement was sometimes provided by the arrival of distinguished visitors. "The Prince of Wales & the Princess arrived here about 11.45" and "The Emperor of Brazil came down here yesterday" – both in July 1871. There were also some invitations out. On 9th July 1871 Richard wrote home:

> I have been very gay of late. I went (1st) For dinner to the Byrons on Thursday, (2nd) Breakfast to Mr. Watson my form master on Friday. (3rd) Breakfast to the Boothby's on Saturday. (4th) I am going to tea to another home boarder this evening.

Harold FitzHerbert at Mr. Clark's in Horncastle in 1876 had a more limited range of outings. He told his Aunt Judith:

> I and Mr. Clark went to a missionary meeting at a place called Goulceby last Tuesday week. I liked it very much, we had tea at Mr. Tyrrel's the clergyman there... It was very kind of you to say I might have an Easter treat. M. Clark thinks of taking me to Lincoln to see the Cathedral and all the old buildings as it is a very cheap journey and very interesting.

George Strutt's pastimes

In the 1890s George Strutt found a great variety of out-of-class activities, both at his Prep. School in Elstree and at Harrow. In May 1889 he wrote home to get permission to take swimming, and in July he reported:

> The baths began yesterday   it is awful fun   there is a spring board over the bath   it is such fun to jump off it.

In December there was skating and, in March 1890, rugby, when he celebrated a "match against harpingdon   it was 19 on our side o on theirs". In November 1891 he described the football field with some enthusiasm, as being "...in a fearful state, you sink nearly up to your knees in mud".

Newly arrived at Harrow in 1892 George mused, "Shall I join the Harrow rifle corps this term? I think perhaps it would be best not, this term, because it interferes with work so much". He did join later, however, for on 6th November 1893 he wrote:

> It was awfully nice at the field day on Wednesday, we went to Hatfield for it … there were about 600 others besides ourselves, all other Public School corps.

In April 1894 he had "passed my shooting with the Morris-tube yesterday, and will be able to go to the proper range as soon as it opens". The following week he wrote, "We had a field day with the Royal Artillery; & some Dragoons & the Household Brigade", giving his usual mark of approval, "It was awful fun". In November 1895 he announced that his House had come second in the Shooting Cup, and, even more exciting, "We are going to have a night attack with the Corps soon".

He enjoyed other aspects of Harrow life too. Soon after his arrival there he wrote to his mother:

> We had House singing last Saturday   it was rather fun. First of all we all had to sing a solo then we had a lot of other songs. [The significance of 'rather fun' instead of 'awful fun' is debatable]. …as we have begun fires we buy tins of cocoa & sugar, condensed milk & cups and brew cocoa in our rooms at night. [He embroidered this picture of revelry in a later letter]. We brew cocoa and chocolate up in our room   it is such fun, but we simply flood the room with condensed milk. [But that was written to his sister Adela].

George was also able to keep pets, though the first ones mentioned, in May 1893, were rather exotic and of doubtful legality. "I have lost an Italian & a German snake in the House & expect they will get spotted by Hallam [his Housemaster] or someone". He next tried something more acceptable; "a pair of sweet little piebald mice … one is fawn and white and the other grey and white". Sadly, little more than a month later he told Adela, "I had 2 awfully nice little dormice here but they have both died".

There is a certain air of surreality about the reference to his next pet, a monkey. There is no mention of it before 11th March 1894. Then it featured in every letter home. (One can only guess at his mother's response to each letter).

11th March

> I will send the monkey home in a hamper as Isabel seems to want it, it is a very tame one, quite young.

16th April

> Has the monkey been advertised for yet? I expect not, I will try to get someone here to buy it if possible.

23rd April

> If the monkey has not been given to Granny or sold yet, I can get a home for it here.

30th April

> How does Granny like the monkey? & how does it like its new home?

29th October

> How is Granny? Please give my love to her. Are the monkeys [!] all right?

There is no further reference to a monkey.

By the 1890s some kind of craftwork was becoming common in Public Schools, partway between proper lessons and games. At Elstree George Strutt netted a hammock. At Harrow in November 1892 he wrote home:

> Some of the boys in the workshop are making canoes, awfully nice ones. There are about twenty making toboggans, and a great many making models of steam yachts about five feet long.

On 10th December 1893 he announced, "I have just finished your Christmas present down at the workshops", but did not say what it was. In March 1894 he made a hutch which he seems to have designed himself, judging by the sketch he put in with his letter.

George also enjoyed the occasional lecture or concert which was arranged for the older pupils. In October 1895 "Sir William Conway came down here & lectured on the Himalayas   some of the lantern slides were beautiful". In November the Bishop of London spoke on "Police Court Missions"; an Old Harrovian gave a talk on "the Atlas Mountains, with a magic lantern" and at the end of the month, "We had a very good concert... Mr. Fred. Dawson, the best

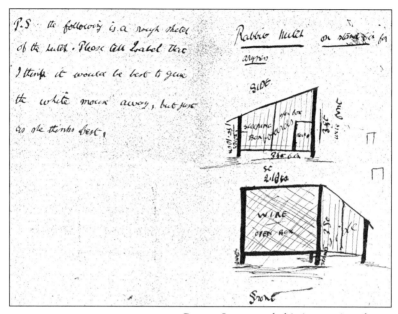

George Strutt sends his instructions home

piano player in England ... and Mr. Andrew Black, the best bass, sang".

Some Derbyshire boys learned to play a musical instrument while at school, or continued with lessons they had already started. In 1798 young Richard Arkwright, at Eton, mentioned, "My flute master is paid by the month ... pray send an order". A letter from William Turbutt in 1867, when he was at Harrow, informed his mother, "I have got a book of voluntaries to play on the organ... I have my lesson on the organ once a week". In another letter he reported, "I am going to learn some of Mozart's Sonatas". When George Strutt went to Elstree he kept up with the violin lessons he had begun at home. In 1891 he wrote, "I am having piano lessons and am in the violin auchestra so on Mondays and Thursdays I have 2 hours music".

Girls' Pastimes

Leisure time in Girls' Schools was very different, because their formal lessons were not taken quite so seriously and any kind of violent exercise or game was regarded as quite unacceptable. Dr. Darwin, in 1797, was prepared to allow "playing at ball, at shuttlecock, swinging and dancing", but no "other modes of exertion". Elizabeth Bradshaw mentioned outings when she was at the Miss Stubbs' school in Wirksworth when she was seven. "Now and then we had tea at the Hurts, and now and then went with our schoolfellows the Arkwrights to Willersley". The only exercise provided by the school was that perennial standby, walking. "We usually walked out to Wirksworth Moor, now [1879] enclosed but then wild & covered with heather &c."

Later, when she was at Miss Murphy's finishing school in Doncaster in 1814, she and her teenage school-fellows were dressed in

> Scarlet Cloth Pelisses, with scarlet Velvet down the fronts from narrow about to broad below, collars, cuffs & epaulets, black Beaver hats & Feathers ... we looked like a detatchment of Army recruits.

Visiting friends took them to the races in Autumn, and Miss Murphy treated them to the theatre in batches of six, when the York Theatrical Company visited Doncaster in December.

Tuck and Grub

One way of filling in spare time pleasantly was eating – not the meals provided by the schools (which are mentioned briefly, but appropriately, in the next Chapter on Parents' Anxieties), but sweets, cakes and other goodies.

The only reference in any of the FitzHerbert boys' letters is in a letter from Richard, dated 30th September 1821, when he remarked, "Notty the tuck man has his place at the further extremity of Wilderness". Hampers of food from home are never mentioned.

In 1846 John Lace had this to say about tuck at Bromsgrove:

> The only & the worst way of spending money here is in eating... A woman and boy from the best confectioners in the town comes up every day with hot pork pies, buns, cheesecakes & all sorts of good things & then on half holidays you can [have] any made or cooked in the town at the shop.

After three more years at Bromsgrove, now in the Sixth Form and heading for Oxford, John seems to have accepted the tradition of extra food. In November 1849 he wrote to Fanny:

> It is the custom for those ... who have been here some time ... to give a supper at the confectioner's which you may suppose is good and expensive. I aspire to nothing of that sort but I thought I might give a small spread to 6 or 8 of my friends in my study ... those pies which I have sometimes brought with me from home have been much liked. I mean the Christmas pies, could you, do you think, send me one, or anything in that way...?

William and Richard Turbutt made no mention of tuck while in Brighton. It is likely that Mr. and Mrs. Kemball Cook did not permit it. When William arrived at Harrow he soon wrote, "I suppose you know what sort of grub to send in my hamper. If you do not, will you please write". And in a P.S. just to be quite sure, "Please write and tell me what you are going to send & also when it is coming". In a letter the next year Richard wrote:

> The grub arrived all safe. We like it all very much. We shall not want chickens another quarter as the fellows bring back such lots of grub with them.

On the subject of tuck, George Strutt takes the biscuit. From Elstree or Harrow, from 1889 to 1895 his letters are full of references to sweets, jam, hampers of food, cakes and so forth. On 3rd June 1890 he wrote to tell his mother of the contents of a hamper he had received, not from home, obviously, from Fortnum's perhaps. There were queen cakes, potted meats, strawberry jam, apricot jam, greengage jam and marmalade. In October the same year he reported:

> Granny sent me a hamper, it had 4 pots of jam, 4 pots of potted meat, 1 pot of anchovy sauce, 1 cake, 12 Norfolk pippins, 1 tin of sardines.

Disasters sometimes happened, as in September 1891: "The hamper came all right except the jam is all over the place".

On 22nd May 1893 at Harrow he begged, "Please send me some more jam and biscuits, sardines &c., just to go on with as all the grub in the House seems to have been devoured". As well as his hampers, his sisters frequently sent him sweets and chocolates – but he also sent them some of their favourite goodies in return.

Parents' Anxieties

> There was a fellow … blew his eye out and both his thumbs with gunpowder… There was a fellow run away a day or two ago…
>
> P.S. Two more fellows got the Scarlet Fever to-day.

– John FitzHerbert at Harrow, 1834.

Nutrition

Recommendation by other parents, personal guarantees by teachers and reassurances in their children's letters were not always enough to allay parents' concerns about the health and safety of their boys and girls away at school.

Food was obviously an important factor. Erasmus Darwin gave very clear advice in his book on Female Education, 1797. He recommended milk, but declared that

> …to take off the cream once, or even twice, as is practised in some boarding schools, before it is given to the children is a shameful circumstance of parsimony, and very injurious to their healths.

If they could not digest milk they should have

> gruel, or tea with cream and sugar in it, and with bread and butter [for breakfast. For supper he suggested] a slice of cold meat, or of cheese or tart, or bread and butter, with small beer or water for drink. [Dinner should consist of] meat plain dress'd with vegetables or bread; and pudding of wheat flour, milk and eggs, with sugar or butter, are more nourishing than vegetable sustenance alone.

Elizabeth Bradshaw's food at the Miss Stubbs' school in Wirksworth in 1805 fell rather short of Dr. Darwin's standards. She recollected:

> Our fare was not inviting – for breakfast skimmed milk with oatmeal thrown in broadcast & came out slimy lumps unboiled inside, & sometimes a snail or earthworm would be found, which got in, in the Cellar where the milk was kept. Coarse meat & Puddings for dinner, sloppy tea and thick bread & scrape for tea. And for supper a small piece of bread and a mite of hard cheese.

Writing about her school food in Doncaster eight years later she remembered, "Our food was plentiful and wholesome and between breakfast & dinner we had dry bread handed round which we were glad of, and liked it".

Comfort

Parents also worried about the warmth and comfort of their children, though the children themselves often accepted discomfort as part of the nature of things. Elizabeth Bradshaw, writing at the age of 81, mentioned two scary experiences she had at her school in Wirksworth, both still vivid memories:

> In the upper corner [of the garden] was a useful retreat – the opening in the seats for grown persons only. On one occasion I slipped – nearly doubled up – my head and heels alone saved me from going down into the town sewer. Another time I somehow provoked the anger of a wild Irish girl who pursued me with a penknife and said, "Now you little gudgeon I have caught you and will cut your throat" and she drew the knife across, but only left her mark.

Of discomforts at her school in Doncaster she mentioned only the coldness of the rooms, a point Richard FitzHerbert also remarked on at Charterhouse in October 1819. "...we find it rather cold in the morning before breakfast". Alleyne was more reassuring in November 1830. "We have had fires nearly all this quarter and so it is pretty cozy. Three fires for about 40 fellows". There were other discomforts. In July 1826 Richard wrote to his father to say he had seen William's new writing desk [William was then at Cambridge] which had

> ...as many secret drawers as there are fleas in my bed, one of which however I have just apprehended & hung 'in terrorem' without the formality of a trial.

In his part of the same letter Alleyne mentioned fagging, which was to become a major feature of Public School life – to some, merely an authorised system of bullying. Alleyne had no worries about it, however, as he wrote, "The upper boys have fagues ... & Dick's fagues are myself and my crony. We have not a great deal to do but Dick gives us tea or coffee every morning & evening". Frederic

Arkwright at Eton in 1820, was less happy about fagging. He asked his mother, "When you write pray tell me about bathing, for all the boys bathe, and if you don't bathe of your own accord, the 5th Form fag you to do it".

Poor food, bullying and other unpleasantnesses were sometimes unbearable. On 5th April 1820 D'Ewes Coke confided to his Diary:

> Sent Edward back to Repton – poor little fellow resembles myself in always having a heavy heart at leaving home for school.

He referred to the same problem later in 1820:

13 August

> Sent Edward to meet the Mail at Dronfield to return to Repton, but it was full and he came back again. [Was it?]

14 August

> Edward went again to Dronfield & obtained a place. He was very sorrowful at going & I found him in bed on Saturday night & on Sunday morning crying – he was better this morning.

To escape some of the annoyances of communal living, senior boys might obtain a study. This practice became increasingly common during the nineteenth century. Anthony FitzHerbert, at Harrow in 1833, refers to it as somewhat of a novel idea. He asked his father:

> I want to know whether you will lend me and John a pound between us to buy a study which is much better than doing your stuff in your rooms because fellows are coming in and out all day.

John Lace wrote to his sister from Bromsgrove in March 1846:

> I am going to try & get a study at Easter ... now I can only work while the rest do, when I get a study I can 'swot' without end.

He went on to mention another hazard which mercifully few schoolboys succumbed to – overwork. Of "two in the VI Form who swot most awfully", he confided, "I am sure one of them will injure his health, he never comes out, I have not seen him in the play ground this half except going to meals and prayers".

By February 1847 he and his chum had got a study:

> Our study is getting pretty comfortable, we have got a thick
> drugget with a pattern like a carpet, & a very neat rug, it is a nice
> light room ... we are to have a washing stand put up today, also a
> blind... I think a candle without a blind looks very dismal. Thorold
> has brought a very nice inkstand ... he is expecting a candle lamp
> soon, so we shall be quite set up.

Much more comfortable than the schoolroom! He went on to ask
Fanny to tell Mama that his chilblains were just starting – not because
of getting his feet wet (which he had, no doubt, been warned about),
"but I suppose it is sitting in school with cold feet".

Frederic Arkwright also mentioned a minor ailment when he was at
Seagrave in 1816. "There is a tetter coming on my face which is very
tiresome but I dare say it will not last long". Again at Eton in 1820, "I
have a small tetter on my face but otherwise quite well".

Illness and Injury

Chilblains, spots and other minor complaints were matters of some
maternal concern, real illness was a greater worry. Children were
usually anxious to reassure their parents. William FitzHerbert made
light of his own and Richard's illness at Charterhouse in July 1819:

> Dick was very ill, but I can assure you that he is quite well. I was
> very ill from Thursday till Monday. I staid in bed two days... I
> lived very well while I was ill. I had a pottle of strawberries for
> breakfast, cherry and currain tart for dinner   they did not allow
> me meat for dinner.

In June 1821 Richard wrote:

> William was taken ill this morning ... it first begun with a very bad
> headache and violent pains in his side. Mrs. Smart gave him a
> black dose, which when he had, occasioned a very great [blank] in
> the stomach, so much so that whatever he has eaten he has thrown
> up except a bason of tea which remained in his stomach.

On another William wrote what was meant to be a reassuring letter
about Richard:

2nd February 1824

> I believe Dick is pretty well but some of the boys say he is very

yellow. Mr. Chapman [their Housemaster] told me that it was a billious attack but he would not allow me to go and see him as the Doctor had particularly ordered that no boy should go there. Mr. Chapman says that nothing was the matter, but he always says nobody is ill without he is very bad. I dare say he will be better soon. I will write on Tuesday or Wednesday.

Your affte. Son,

W. FitzHerbert

On reading though what he had written he decided that it was somehow not quite reassuring enough, so he added, "I do not think he is very bad".

He was bad enough, however, to be taken from school to the FitzHerbert house at Farleigh in Kent, to the relief of his great-uncle, Lord St. Helens, who wrote to Lady Agnes that he "rejoiced to hear of his arrival, and I trust that you will keep him with you till quite re-established. Of all the minor diseases the jaundice being the most obstinate and most apt to return".

Alleyne joined his elder brothers at Charterhouse at the beginning of June. Only a couple of weeks later William had some bad news for his mother: "Dear Alleyne is now in bed… He has had a black dose & it has operated 2 or 3 times. He has coughed up some phlegm, but he seems to breathe better and easier".

Four days later Lady Agnes wrote to Sir Henry, who was staying in London, "I am in the greatest distress about our dear child". To her great relief there was better news in a few days, but she wrote to tell her husband of her anxiety. "Nanny & I were packed & prepared to set out … as no one can nurse like a Mother". She wondered whether Alleyne should be taken away from school, "as he is not yet inured to its hardships" and whether he should be given some of "the old Rhubarb mixture". Happily for Alleyne, he recovered quite soon.

It was always worrying when a child wrote home mentioning some epidemic going through the school. In 1823 Richard FitzHerbert reported, "The houping cough is in the school   four boys have got it".

Far more alarming was John FitzHerbert's letter to his father from Harrow on 21st November 1834:

Half the fellows out of this House are gone, or going, home, because of the Scarlet Fever. There was a fellow at Longlery's [House] the other night blew his eye out and both his thumbs with gunpowder. I believe he is going to have one of his thumbs cut off and is going to have something done to his eye ... by Brodie [surgeon] who is to come from London. There was a fellow run away a day or two ago, only he was stopped when he got to Barnet.

P.S. Two more fellows got the Scarlet Fever to-day.

Injuries from accidents or fights were other possibilities. For much of the 19th century masters exercised very little supervision over the boys outside lesson time, and it was generally accepted that a new boy would have a 'battle' shortly after his arrival at boarding school. In July 1819 William FitzHerbert wrote to his sister Selina, proudly reporting, "I have fought one battle   we neither of us licked   I got a black eye and he got a black nose   we were about equal".

Sometimes an incident occurred at school which caused parents great anxiety even though their own children were not directly involved. Lady Agnes sent Sir Henry a detailed account of "a most heart-rending event" at Eton in March 1825, in which a 14-year-old son of Lord Shaftesbury and a son of Colonel Wood had "quite a regular battle like the Boxers". Shaftesbury's son was given "more than half a pint" of brandy to keep him going, but he collapsed, and died about an hour later. It was, as Lady Agnes commented, "a sad, sad story".

William Turbutt's mother must have been appalled to read his letter of 13th February 1867:

The accident of the shooting happened in this manner. One of the boys had a revolver which he had been accustomed to shoot with and the evening on which the accident occurred, the Head of the House had told him not to do so. He then amused himself in shooting off caps. He, however, knew that one barrel was loaded but did not think that he would come to it so soon. He stupidly was looking down the barrel when he fired the caps and the charge going off, the bullet went in between his eye and nose.

He died the next day.

Tragedies like these led to more supervision of leisure hours, more organised games and activities and a greater alertness to danger on the part of school staff.

George Strutt's Ailments

From the 1820s to the 1890s contact between parents and children at school was improved in a number of ways. Travel by rail was much faster than by coach. Penny Post letters were usually delivered within a day or two, and telegrams arrived within hours of being sent. Parents still had the feeling, however, of being remote from their children, and unable to contact them quickly enough in the event of accident or illness.

In George's second month at Elstree, he told his mother an amusing story, but she probably did not think it as much of a 'lark' as he did:

> We had such fun in dormitory the other night. There are rats in it & they have got a hole through the floor so last night as soon as we heard them come out we covered the hole up and shied books at them, and nearly got cobbed by the dormitory master as we made such a row.

Accidents mostly happened to other boys, but George did complain, in May 1890, how "The other day I had got my hand on a glass & it bust & cut my hand a little".

It probably did not help his mother to enjoy her stay in Scotland in 1891 when she heard:

> One of the boys nearly broke his nose   he was in the gymnasium and fell down from the top his nose is bent all on one side of his face and is double its size and he has got two black eyes.

Nor was it reassuring to be told the next year, "Yesterday a boy got his front teeth knocked out by a cricket ball".

George's first experience of school illness was mumps. On 5th June 1891 Mrs. Sanderson, the wife of the Headmaster at Elstree, wrote to Mrs. Strutt, saying "Georgie has sort of 'pretence mumps' – they are very little". And adding that she was "sending the few cases we have to the Sick Cottage". The pretence, however, turned to reality, and when George wrote again about a fortnight later it was to say, "I am nearly well now but still up at the cottage". By 23rd June he was back at school, but reported "11 chaps with the mumps" and on 30th "34 chaps with the mumps". The next year chicken pox struck, but George escaped it.

George at Harrow

When he got to Harrow, at first everything went well. He shared a study with two other boys and informed his mother:

> Boys are allowed pictures and things in our rooms. I am making the room I am in very smart. I have bought a tablecloth and 2 cushions, 1 canvas chair, a lot of fans and photo frames & brackets, pictures and ornaments and a nice inkstand. The other boys are making the room smart too. I am going to be fag to a boy called Porter   he is brother to the Porter in my room and is very nice.

In November 1895 there was more disturbing news, that "a chap in our House last night got his nose broken in three places in a fight". A letter from Hallam, the Housemaster, to George's parents, and his mother's subsequent request for an explanation from George, led to a fuller account of the affair:

> The 'discreditable teasing' that Hallam talks of was this. About four of us used to 'ragg' Hunt in quite a mild way, and never to hurt him, it was chiefly setting 'booby traps' which he always found out... One night another chap, whom I personally 'bar', came up and started ragging Hunt... Hunt made for him & they had a fight & the other chap broke Hunt's nose... Hallam wanted to know who had ever ragged Hunt, so we all got a Sixth Form whopping. I am sorry ... and shall take care not to let it happen again.

The most worrying times for George's parents were in 1893 and 1894, when he had two attacks of 'flu followed by other ailments. In January 1893 George wrote home, mentioning that "Hallam puts my headache down to my polk [pork] pie & I expect will write and tell you not to send another". On 15th February there was a report from Mrs. Hallam that George's temperature was about 100 [Fahrenheit], "but his pulse has dropped from 97 to 70". The next day a terse note came from Margaret Ross, the Matron. "Mr. Strutt is not allowed any fruit excep [sic] Grapes & Oranges. I will take care of the box until he is better".

Five telegrams were sent over the period 15th to 17th February, giving George's temperature, and Mrs. Hallam wrote reassuring Mrs. Strutt that George's influenza was "an extremely mild attack" and reassuring her (a little sharply, perhaps?):

> Thank you for offering to send a nurse, we have 8 boys ill & have someone who devotes her time entirely to them – and it is not in the slightest necessary.

At last, early in March, George was able to write, "The influenza is all right in the school now".

It reappeared in December 1893. George told his mother, "…only one case in our House though… I hope I don't get the influenza, it will be rot if I do". But he did. On 16th December Mrs. Hallam wrote, "I know you will be sorry to hear that George has influenza… His temperature this morning was just over 103… It is most trying for George just at the end of term". Two days later she wrote again, quoting the doctor as saying that George was well enough to travel home. (She had previously sent a telegram to the Strutts addressed: Makeney, Duffield, only to have it "returned to sender" from Driffield, in Yorkshire).

She wrote again on 20th to say that his temperature was now over 99 and he would have to stay at the school over Christmas. All the other boys had gone, so he would be the doctor's only patient, and "the Matron who is most devoted to the boys is now free to attend to him herself". She and her husband, she explained, "have engagements for spending Christmas at Shrewsbury".

George's father travelled to see him on 22nd bringing some presents from home and bringing back a long letter, five pages, from George:

> Dear Mother,
>
> Thank you very much for all the beef tea, grapes, etc., you have sent me… It is very nice daddy being here… I feel perfectly well and in excellent spirits, so don't worry about me. It is so tiresome not being able to buy my Christmas presents for Adela, Isabel and the babies.

Mrs. Ross, he said, was very kind, and had given him

> An egg for breakfast this morning and a custard pudding for lunch,
> & tea & bread & butter for tea.

His father returned home that evening, but George wrote again on 23rd and again on Christmas Day, saying "I was up nearly the whole day today. I had my Christmas with Mrs. Ross in grand style". His father went to Harrow again on Boxing Day to bring George home, but had to delay, because, as he wrote, "Dr. Blindloss [the name was actually Bindloss] said he must not be removed till midday as the morning air would be bad for him". George had reported feeling a bit ill on Christmas Day, but his father explained, "It must have been a bit of indigestion for he had turkey, blackcock & plumb pudding for dinner". [Obviously what George meant by "grand style"].

George Strutt could count himself lucky not to have been a pupil at Abbotsholme. Dr. Cecil Reddie, the founder, declared in 1900 that in the previous ten years there had been no serious, or even trivial, illness among the pupils at his school. He did admit that there had been influenza "brought back by some after the Christmas vacation", but although about a dozen boys caught it, "all got over it in three or four days without any outside help whatever". And he went on to remark, rather tartly, "The boys are taught to see ... that disease is the result of error, ignorance, overwork, misapplied work, or vice".

Dr. Bindloss's treatments may not have been very effective, but at least he did not think that it was George's own fault, having 'flu, and that he should get over it himself.

By the end of January 1894 George was back at school, but still not very well. Mrs. Hallam reported that he had styes, and added, a little unkindly, "I am so sorry he should have come back like this – but no doubt the change here will do him good". Throughout February George suffered:

> It hurts awfully to have them [the styes] lanced... as soon as one goes another comes... I have only been allowed to go up to school two days this term... I have got enough cocoa & beef tea to last me some time yet, thanks.

At the end of the month he was complaining:

> I am not allowed to play rackets or anything because of heating my

blood. I believe that Dr. Bindloss does not do my eyes any good, what with lotions and drops and tonic. [One can only agree!]. I have not had the shade off my eye once this term yet... I am not allowed to read.

At last, on 5th March, George wrote to say, "I am allowed out now". The next day Dr. Bindloss himself wrote to Mrs. Strutt:

> Your son is now much better & has no stye in his eyelids at all at present. I have been giving him Iron & Quinine, Burgundy & Porter & a liberal diet & have ordered him to take quiet walks; & I have also put him on to a course of special pills... [He also advised a stay at] some sheltered, but still bracing place on the South Coast. Bournemouth, Hastings or St. Leonards would do; Torquay would be too relaxing.

It seems probable that George did spend some time by the sea, and by 16th April his weekly letters from Harrow began again. Early in July Mrs. Hallam referred to "boils" in a letter to Mrs. Strutt, but since George himself wrote on 18th July to tell how he had gone with a school party to see the Eton v. Harrow match at Lord's, we may assume that he had got rid of the boils fairly quickly. His frequent references, later in 1894 and in 1895, to Field Days with the Rifle Corps and other activities, show that his unhappy times of illness did not recur.

"School", built perhaps by Wren in 1683–87: The North front
(from Hawkes: Winchester College)

Stanfree Infants School, Bolsover

PART 2: Schools for the Poor

Sunday Schools and Day Schools before 1870

> Some ... appliances might be used with success, especially a Blackboard.

– Report of School Inspector, 1855.

Sunday Schools

The idea of Sunday Schools for poor children was promoted by Robert Raikes in Gloucester in 1780, and quickly spread. The children of Youlgreave had the opportunity to attend one from September 1801. The well-off townspeople who set it up were quite clear as to their motives:

> ...in consideration of the beneficial tendency of giving instruction to the Children of the Poor & keeping them from contracting idle & mischievous habits on the Sabbath Day...

On weekdays, of course, they would be helping their parents at work or working themselves. The parents were told to see that the children "be wash'd, comb'd & clad as decently as they can afford" or risk being passed over whenever there were any charity handouts.

A master was to be employed "who shall teach them to read (and write if it be thought necessary". There were to be two sessions; the first from nine o'clock until the time for Morning Service in Church, which all scholars were to attend, and the second in the afternoon. There was to be one teacher for every 30 pupils.

Among the expenses recorded over the next few years were for Forms, or benches in 1801, and £1.12s.4d. for "books &c." in 1802. Well-behaved and regular attenders were given "Easter Sunday rewards" which cost 7 shillings, and we may hope that these coloured texts and religious booklets were received with as much delight as the donors expected.

A Sunday School, of course, was not just for religious education – it was a school, on Sunday. The School accounts for later years illustrate this. Between 1805 and 1817 there were purchases of spelling books, easy reading books, writing paper, inkstands and quills.

One of the goals of the Sunday School movement – respectability – was certainly achieved in Derbyshire. In 1842 one of the Parliamentary Commissioners reporting on coal mining in the East of the county recorded that, although the children were very dirty on weekdays, "I was much pleased at the particularly neat and clean appearance of the collier children I met with at the various Sunday Schools".

How the children themselves felt about this is another matter. One man told the Commissioner, "There are Sunday Schools, when they will go; but when boys have been beaten, knocked about, and covered with sludge all the week, they want to be in bed to rest all day on Sunday". A seven-year-old, Thomas Straw of Ilkeston, was just one out of many children who bore this out. He "feels tired and sleepy on a Sunday morning; would rather be in bed than go to school". Small wonder that, with illiterate parents and untrained teachers, children like these made little progress. The Commissioners recorded their backwardness:

> Has been 4 or 5 years to Baptist Sunday School; cannot spell horse or cow.
> Has been to the Methodists' Sunday School, Ripley, 5 years; only reads a, b, ab; cannot spell in the least; cannot tell what d-o-g spells – he says "gun".
> Goes to the Methodist Sunday School, has been there a year; was at Smalley Free School before he worked in the pits; he cannot write; reads in the Bible ... can scarcely spell words of one syllable.

Charity Schools, Factory Schools and Dame Schools

At the same time (1842) the Commissioners investigating conditions in the collieries found the same lack of schooling among other children. The Charity Schools were very small, and restricted by various ancient rules and conditions. At Trowell Free School, for example, 15 places were reserved for children from Woollaton, 10 for children from Trowell itself, and 5 for children from Cossall. Denby

Free School had places for 20 boys and 13 girls. In most schools, if a child could not attend regularly he or she was expelled. At Pinxton Day School children were allowed to attend whenever they were not at work, but the fees were a penny a week for reading, and twopence a week to learn to write.

Children working in textile mills in Derbyshire were among the first to have an opportunity to learn to read and write. In 1785 the Derby Mercury reported on Jedediah Strutt's Sunday School in Belper "for the benefit of all the youth of both sexes employed in his Cotton Mill". In the accounts of the Evans' Mill School at Darley Abbey for the year 1797-1798 there are expenses which clearly indicate lessons in writing as well as reading: a bottle of ink; Books from Pritchard's; Slate pencils. Richard Arkwright also provided a Sunday School for his child workers in Cromford, where a visitor in 1801 noted, in a much-quoted entry in his Diary, they "looked healthy & well ... attended by an Old Man, their School Master".

Of Dame Schools in Derbyshire there is little recorded. In 1728 William Hutton of Derby was sent at the age of five to what could have been a Dame School, except that the teacher was a man, "Mr. Thomas Meat ... who often took occasion to beat my head against the wall, holding it by the hair... I hated all books but those of pictures".

Cruel, unhealthy and ineffective though they were, Dame Schools were cheap and they survived for many years in some places, undercutting the fees of other schools. They finally went out of business after 1891, when elementary education was made free. Their standards were condemned by teachers at other schools. The Headmistress of Melbourne Infants' School recorded in October 1893 that Alice Copley, a very bright seven-year-old, had been put up into the Girls' Department after only four months in the Infants. "She was admitted to this school on the 4th of May 1893 being then very backward, as she had been attending a dame School". In 1894 the Headmistress of Kirkstead Girls' School noted:

> Have admitted two girls, Patty & Ethel Hand, from a private school in the village. They are very deficient in grammar and arithmetic, and read without any expression.

Derbyshire Children at School 1800-1900

A village school – Tissington

Very few day schools before the mid-19th century left much evidence of their existence. Much of the pupils' writing was done on slates; the teacher, the squire and the parson could meet and settle any matters without putting anything down on paper, and the teacher was not required by law to keep any records.

One Derbyshire village school for which some information survives is the school in Tissington – fairly typical of many others. A receipt exists dated 1778, for the teacher's salary:

> Reced of William FitzHerbert Esqr. by the hands of John Tatham fforty Shillings being in full for half a year's Payment for Teaching Shoole   Due to me at Michealmas last
>
> by me Mary X ffletcher

A similar receipt for £4 for the year 1779 was signed by William Fletcher, on behalf of his sister, Mary. It is hard to believe that Mary put a cross on the receipt because she could not write, even to sign her own name.

In 1782 Mary Fletcher died and her place was taken by Ellen Smith, at the same salary, to teach "all such poor children" as were approved by the Squire.

> The Boys to be taught reading & writing, & the Girls to be instructed in reading knitting, & spinning & plain work [sewing].

Notice that the girls were not taught to write and there is no mention of arithmetic.

After seven years, Ellen Smith asked for a better school, daring to complain, in writing, that it was "too Small, dark, Subject to Smoke and every way inconvenient". Nothing was done, however, for nearly fifty years. In 1837 a new school was built with money donated by one of the FitzHerbert family. The Charity fund at this time was still providing only £4 a year for the teacher's salary.

By 1855 there were separate Boys' and Girls' rooms, with a Master, Mr. Stokes, and a Mistress, Miss Gerrard. The then Squire, Sir Henry, asked Mr. Barry, a Government Inspector, to report to him on the state of the school.

Mr. Barry was "extremely pleased" with the building itself, but he recommended that the floor should be boarded. [At the time it was just beaten earth]. He was "extremely dissatisfied" with the general state of the Boys' School. The lowest class spent the whole day

> ...learning their letters & monosyllables, no attempt being made to teach them to count or to write on slates, or any variation made in their work.

Some of these boys, in the lowest class, were already nine or ten years old.

In the next class "they were unable to repeat the line of three in the multiplication table". Religious knowledge was "miserably small" and some boys, even in the top class, "cannot read intelligibly". Part of the cause of such backwardness is suggested by the daily attendance figures. Of 40 boys on the register, the usual daily attendance was 17 and the average for the previous year was 19.

The girls had just as little opportunity to learn. Miss Gerrard told the Inspector that "the cold is almost unbearable, that some parents refuse to send their children during the Winter thro' dread of it". This was in spite of the fact that the pupils contributed "coal money" and Miss Gerrard herself gave £2.5s.0d. out of her £25.15s.0d. a year salary.

Mr. Barry suggested that "some of the numberless appliances of an Infants School might be used with success, especially a Blackboard".

Out of 41 girls, only 18 could do "any sort of Sum in Arithmetic". Some girls could repeat the Church of England Catechism, but "none seemed to understand the meaning of the words". The girls' attendance was as poor as the boys'. Their daily average for the year was 17. The Inspector also objected to the use of the Bible and Prayer Book "as their exclusive class-book". Both the boys and the girls paid weekly fees, ranging from fourpence down to a penny. Ten of the girls from very poor families paid nothing. The Inspector made no complaint about the fact that while £4.5s.8d. was spent each year on "books and apparatus" for the boys, the amount spent in the girls' department was only 9 shillings.

The quality of the teaching, the poor attendance, and the lack of books and equipment, especially in the Girls' school, were quite usual for the time, but the FitzHerberts decided that real improvements were needed. In 1857 two new teachers, man and wife, were appointed and Sir Henry undertook to make their joint salary up to £80 a year. In 1858 Lady Agnes drew up a book of Rules for the Tissington School. This handwritten notebook contains sixty rules, as much for the teachers' and parents' guidance as for the pupils.

A scale of fees was laid down which classified parents from Farmers down to labourers. Farmers had to pay 6 pence a week each for their two eldest children, and 4 pence each for any younger ones. Tradespeople paid 6 pence each for the first two, and 3 pence for any others. Tradespeople "not in constant employ" paid 4 pence and 2 pence, and servants paid 3 pence and 1 penny on the same basis. Labourers paid only one penny a week for each child. The School Pence were to be paid every Monday, and the Master was to report any child who came without money, so that, if there were good reasons, the child would be allowed to attend school free.

There were two school sessions: nine o'clock to twelve and two o'clock until four. This gave children living outside the village two hours to walk home for dinner and walk back. Children who lived at a distance from the school were to be allowed home half an hour early, but only "during the months of January, November and December when the day is dark or stormy". During lesson times "The Children to be allowed a few minutes play in the open air, by Classes in turn. The Boys not to be allowed to go out at the same time with the Girls". And they were not to play in the Churchyard. The only excuse accepted for absence was "real, well-known sickness".

Almost every possible incident and occasion was covered by a rule in some detail. The school day was to begin "with Prayer and reading the Holy Scriptures" and the children were "to kneel down very quietly" at Prayers, according to Rule 14. Only farmers were expected to pay for their children's textbooks, but even "Charity Children" had to pay for copy-books. New copy-books were not kept in the school, but at the Hall. To get a new one a pupil had to hand in the full copy-book at the Hall "after Morning School on Tuesdays and call again for a new one on Wednesdays before Morning School". By Rule 19 "The Head Girl & Boy of each Class [is to] receive the Pens & Pencils after the Lesson is over & return the Boxes to the Master or Mistress".

The School also functioned as a Sunday School, but attendance does not appear to have been compulsory. Rule 56, however, promised "Rewards" to the six best attenders at the end of each year. Cleanliness being next to Godliness, the pupils were required to sweep and dust the schoolroom and to wash dusters and towels. Girls were to wear clogs coming to school "or else to bring with them a pair of clean shoes to wear in the School". Rule 43 was "To encourage the Labourer's children to wear plain Caps under their bonnets with plain fronts, and neat ribbands for their bonnets". Presumably, such high standards of cleanliness and neatness could not be expected from the boys.

Readers may recognise echoes of their own schooldays from some of these rules. Everyone will probably remember being told as a pupil that, as Rule 50 stated, Rules were made for their benefit.

Unwillingly to School

> I find the children very rough & ignorant – a great many of them have never been to school before.

– The Headmistress of a Girls' School, January 1878.

Board Schools

Twelve years after the Tissington School Rules were drawn up the School Boards began their work and many children found their lives suddenly changed, not always to their satisfaction. Some, or course, knew school, but only as an occasional experience. Many had never been to school, and it took time for them to understand what they could expect and what was expected of them. In a great many cases, neither parents nor elder brothers or sisters had gone to school, and so could not tell these children what school was like. They were somewhat unwilling pioneers of literacy in Derbyshire.

Even where the pupils had been at school before, as at Pinxton, for example, the Head recorded in October 1876, "Writing was very imperfect in all except the 1st Class, and arithmetic was in a very poor state all through the school". In November "many boys even in the

4

SCHOOL HOURS.

5.—The Schools shall be open for instruction during five days of the week, from 9 a.m. to 12 noon, and from 1-30 p.m. to 4 p.m. This does not prohibit the teacher from extending the time to 5 o'clock, as a punishment for misconduct, or inefficiently prepared lessons.

REGISTRATION.

6.—All Registers and summaries shall be duly closed and entered up every Friday Evening before the teachers leave the School.

7.—The Head Teachers shall be held responsible for the accuracy of all books and returns, but they are at liberty to delegate the keeping of them to subordinates.

8.—Visits of Members and Officers of the Board shall be recorded in the Log Book by the Head Teacher.

TIME TABLES.

9.—The Head Teacher must submit all Time Tables for the approval of the Board, previous to their signature by Her Majesty's Inspector.

5

RELIGIOUS INSTRUCTION.

10.—In such Time Tables provision shall be made for Religious Instruction and observances, to consist of Bible reading, Hymns and Prayers, with such explanations and instructions as are suited to the capacities of children, having strict regard to the provisions of the Education Act in Sections 7 and 14, both in letter and spirit, which stipulate that no attempt be made to attach children to any particular denomination.

11.—The Religious Instruction shall be given by or under the direction of the Head Teacher, and shall be that prescribed in the Printed Scheme of Religious Teaching adopted by the Board.

PUNISHMENT.

12.—Corporal punishment shall not be inflicted except in urgent cases, and then only by the principal teacher who shall be held directly responsible for every punishment of the kind, and shall enter in the Log Book of the School a

6

formal record of every such punishment and the
reason for its infliction.

FEES.

13.—The following scale of weekly fees shall
be paid on the Monday morning, or the first
time in the week that the child attends school :

Infants..1d. each.
Children over 7—Full-time .... 3d. „
   „   „ —Half-time .... 2d. „
If three or more children over 7 from
    one family .... 2d. „
Children who have passed in the 5th
    Standard ....4d. „

14.—Teachers must insist on pre-payment of
the School Fees.

15.—Teachers shall not regard any fees as
remitted without having received the authority
of the Board. When orders for remission of fees
are received, the teacher must enter the letter **R**
in the fees' column of the register, from the

7

commencement of the orders to the exact date to
which they extend.

16.—Applicants for remission of fees should
be referred to the Attendance Officer.

17.—All monies received as fees must be paid
to the Treasurer at the Derby and Derbyshire
Bank not later than 4 o'clock on the last Saturday
in each month, the forms of "Credit Note"
supplied being used.

HALF-TIMERS.

18.—No children shall be allowed to be absent
from School half-time, except those who have
received a "Labour Certificate" from the Board.

19.—Applications for Labour Certificates must
be made to the Clerk of the Board, who is
authorized to grant Certificates if satisfied that
the following regulations prescribed by the
Education Department have been complied with :

1.—The child must have passed the Third
    Standard, and

2.—Must be not less than 10 years of age.

Extract from the regulations
of the Belper School Board

1st class could not shape their letters correctly or copy down a line of print without mistakes". But he added, "Home lessons were worked willingly, and the third class showed quite an enthusiasm to begin". In December, however, discipline had "not been quite so satisfactory, the school being noisy at times, and severe measures required to restore order".

The novelty of homework seems to have worn off by February 1877, when "several have been kept in during the week for careless home lessons". Even as late as April a quiet work routine was not achieved: "Frequently all work has had to be suspended till order was restored".

The Headmistress of Brimington Common School [quoted above] still found her girls "very backward" in February, but by March they were "improving in order but still not so orderly as I could wish".

Some 'pioneers' were late starting on the road to literacy. In July 1891, 21 years after the School Boards were set up and 11 years after school attendance was made compulsory, the Brimington Common School Log Book records, "Admitted two new scholars, one nine years old & never been to school before".

One feature of school which children did not like was having to stay there for a fixed number of hours every day. It was a long day for children as young as four, who might also have a long walk to and from school. At Pinxton in 1876 the hours were 9.00 a.m. to 12 noon, and 1.30 p.m. to 4.00. Belper School Board set the same times in 1886, and they were, in fact, usual throughout the County.

Head Teachers could vary the School Day a little for special reasons. In early January 1889 the pupils at Melbourne Infants' School were "...dismissed five minutes earlier in the afternoons this week, owing to dense fogs, as many of the little ones live some distance from School". At Kirkstead Girls', in January 1892, the Headmistress noted, "As many of the girls are compelled to go to the colliery office for their fathers' wages before 4 p.m. every Friday I have commenced afternoon school at 1 p.m. instead of at 1.15 and have closed at 3.30". At Hartington, school finished at 4.15 in the summer, but at 3.30 in the winter.

School Fees

One important feature of school life was the fee or "school pence" which had to be handed over to the teacher every Monday morning until 1890, when elementary education was made free by Act of Parliament. The fee was a source of potential embarrassment for children whose parents were judged by the authorities to be very poor. These children did not have to pay and therefore stood out from the rest. If paying parents were temporarily short of cash and sent their children to school without the money, they were sent home to get it, again feeling ashamed, and missing some lessons.

There was always a chance that a child might lose or spend the money before reaching school, or perhaps decide not to go to school at all. This could explain the case of James Broomhead of Hartington, in September 1889, who was "Sent home in the afternoon for his School Fees". In October he was in trouble for "playing away from School" and a year later, on 14th October 1890 "The Attendance Officer ... made enquiry about James Broomhead who had habitually played away from school".

Even children under the age of seven might be sent home for fees. At Melbourne Infants', on 1st September 1887, "Alice Poxon and Pollie

This is believed to be a Derbyshire school. Does anyone know where?

Robey sent home at 9.15 for their school money, neither returned".
On 19th January 1888, "Two children sent home this afternoon for
school pence, neither returned". An entry in the School Log Book in
February 1889 explains the reason: "I have had great difficulty this
week in getting some of the school pence... A great many of the
children's parents are out of work".

At Pinxton in February 1877 the Head noted, "...many parents are
working short time ... the fees were not paid so punctually ... the
arrears amount to 5s.6d.". In July he accounted for the low
attendance as caused by "parents' inability to pay the fees and
reluctance to make application for remittance".

Inability to pay, reluctance to ask for "charity", missing days or
weeks of schooling: these were all sources of anxiety and ill-feeling to
parents, and to those children who wanted to do well at school and
better themselves.

School fees varied through being set by different School Boards, and
also according to the ages of the pupils and other factors. At
Hartington in 1868 farmers' children paid more than others, and
children over ten had to pay slightly more than under-tens. A farmer's
child over ten years old paid 8d. per week. In 1879 at Brimington
Common the fees were under-sevens 2d., over sevens 3d. At Pinxton
the fees were the same as these for children who lived in the parish,
but 4d. for outsiders of any age.

In 1880 the Belper School Board published a quite complex Scale of
Fees:

Under seven	1d. per week
Over seven (full time)	3d. per week
Over seven (half time)	2d. per week
Children of Fifth Standard	6d. per week

If three or more children over seven of the same family were attending
school at the same time, each paid only 2d. per week. To qualify as a
half time pupil, a child had to be ten or over and must have passed
Third Standard. (This was the usual achievement for nine- or ten-
year-old children). The Board also had to be convinced that the
family was in real need of the child's wages. He or she was then
issued with a Labour Certificate and was only required to attend five
of the school's ten weekly sessions.

All this may seem unnecessarily complicated, but the variety of fees and the apparently small gradations between them underline their real significance to parents with only moderate or low incomes. To have one or two children reach a point at which the fees increased could dent the weekly budget badly. On the other hand, to have a child going to school only half time, with lower fees and able to earn some money at work, would mean a significant improvement in the family's income.

Holidays

One pleasant aspect of school which children (not to mention teachers) welcomed was holidays. The holidays listed in the Belper School Board's Regulations for 1891 were as follows: Shrove Tuesday afternoon; Good Friday and all of Easter Week; Whit-week; four weeks during July; two weeks at Christmas. These were typical of most Derbyshire schools at the time, but there were some local variations.

In many places the children's attachment to local Wakes, Feasts and other traditional holidays proved stronger than the school authorities. In 1878 the Head of Pottery Boys' School in Belper wrote in his Log Book, "Oct. 28th Belper Fair Week a thin attendance in consequence". That was on Monday. A hasty discussion with the Board led to Thursday and Friday being declared Holidays, "being the last two days of Fair". By 1880 advance notice was being given that "the School will be closed for the whole of next week, being Belper Fair week". By 1886 this week's holiday was enshrined in the printed regulations, but even then, as the Head closed the school on the Friday afternoon of the previous week, he noted, "great falling-off in attendance this week probably owing to the Fair being so near".

The children of Brimington Common won the same sort of battle with the authorities. In October 1878 the Head recorded, "Brimington Feast... The School is very poorly attended this week". The following year the authorities put their foot [or feet] down. "Only Monday afternoon after Feast Sunday to be observed as a holiday, by Order...". There is no reliable evidence in the following years as to how many children voted with their feet for a week's holiday, but in 1895 the Board faced facts, accepted defeat, and the School Log records, "October 4th. School closed for a week's

6

1878

Oct. 28th Beeper Fair week a thin attendance in consequence.

" 30th The Board gave a Holiday for (Thursday + Friday) the remainder of the week, being the two last days of Fair.
First Quarter on Registers completed

Nov. 5th Examined Standard II in Arithmetic + Dictation on plates. about 45 pc. passed.

" 8th The Average attendance for the week was 58.8 which is lower than it had been for some time with the exception of last week. The attendance of many of the children is most irregular; there is also a great difficulty in getting them to School in time.

" 11th Isabel Weston - 2nd Year, Transfer Pupil Teacher from Denby Endowed School commenced her duties to day at this School as a Pupil Teacher.

" 13th Punished George Wain for writing bad language on the School Walls

" 18th Master left School at 3-25 on very important business

30

1880

Oct. 29 In accordance with instructions received from the Clerk of the Board, the School will be closed for the whole of next week, being Belper fair week

Nov. 8 Reopened School this morning Messrs Hale & Burrell members of the School Board visited School.

" 19 Examined 2nd Standard in Geography (taught by J Weston P.T.) found them very backward. Also Examined 1st Standard found that the boys who came up from the Infant School with one or two exceptions are very backward indeed several of them do not even know their letters. The average for the week has been 85.6 as against 56.9 for corresponding week last year

" 26 Friday morning very wet this School in Consequence. Only 62 present. Usual work for week Average Attendance 81.6

" 29 Mr. J.B. Tracket Clerk to School Board Visited School this morning.

Pages from the Log Book of Belper Pottery Boys' School

holiday". In 1896 the Feast Week was actually extended to three weeks' holiday, but not all the pupils were happy about that, because it was "...owing to an epidemic of measels".

In some places, however, traditional holidays never gained official recognition. At Hartington, Newhaven Fair Day was regarded by the children as a holiday. Hartington School Log, 30th October 1871, Monday: "Newhaven Fair. Four children only [out of about 80] attended school. Consequently gave a holiday". But even in 1899 the school authorities still held out. "New Haven Fair – poor attendance today".

Sometimes an unexpected day or half-day off delighted the children as much as, or more than, the regular holidays. Children were sometimes given time off school to visit a circus or some other travelling show. Probably schools made a virtue of necessity, as large numbers of children would stay away in any case, with or without their parents' connivance. The Head of Belper Pottery School, on 5th April 1880, found "Only 39 boys present this afternoon [out of about 90], a Circus in the town being the cause".

The Infants at Melbourne were given the afternoon off on 25th September 1885 "owing to Edmond's Wild Beasts' Show coming into the village". In October 1881 the Hartington children had an unexpected half-holiday, "Swallow's Circus being in the place, and a cheap entertainment being given to the children". The girls of Kirkstead School had an organised visit to "Edmond's, late Wombwell's Menagerie" in the afternoon of 9th October 1890, and only three weeks later, "A Half-holiday given because of Fossett's Circus being in the village".

The pupils at Brimington Common had few half-holidays, but in 1899 they had a whole day off on 1st November "owing to a visit of Barnum's and Bailey's Show to Chesterfield". On 1st August some of them had taken unofficial holidays. The entry in the Log Book reads, "A flower show in the neighbourhood & Sabbath School Treat has interfered very much with the attendance during the week".

Visiting a Flower Show was usually treated as an acceptable excuse for absence. In July 1892 the Brimington Common children had "Two days holiday. Ringwood Flower Show & Church Sunday School Treat". At Hartington in 1888 the pupils had a holiday "on account of the Sunday School trip to Dovedale". In 1895 "The Band of Hope children" were allowed to go "to Alstonefield Flower Show" on 15th August, and on 17th August 1898 all the Hartington pupils were dismissed from school at 2.50 so that they could enjoy "Vicar's kind treat to the Alstonefield Show".

Sometimes there were more exciting reasons for a holiday than a Flower Show. On 6th April 1885, the Head of Melbourne Infants' wrote, "Opened School this morning with a fair attendance... Closed School in the afternoon, the attendance being so poor owing to a Review taking place in the village". At the end of June 1873 the Hartington children were allowed a whole day off to see "the Volunteer inspection at Bakewell". And in 1874 they had a holiday in August, to the delight of the boys, with their wooden swords and paper caps, "to witness the Sham Fight between the Hartington and Ashbourne Volunteers".

Events of national importance might also be marked by a school holiday. On 6th July 1893 the schoolchildren in Melbourne were treated to a free tea to celebrate "The Royal Wedding Day". On 15th June 1897 the Rev. Canon Singleton presented the School with a picture of the Queen, and on the 18th the importance of the Diamond Jubilee was even more firmly impressed on the children by giving them a whole week's holiday.

Unusually, in August 1894 the Kirkstead pupils had a holiday for no particular reason, but simply, as the Log Book records:

> ...in order to give the children a treat. The day being fine, the children enjoyed themselves in a field during the afternoon, returned to school for tea which had been prepared by the teachers during the morning, then again went back to the field during the evening when various sports were indulged in, the prizes won in these being afterwards distributed by the Chairman of the Board.

An early example of the School Sports Day, but not, perhaps, as touching as the note made by the Head of Melbourne Infants' School on 1st May 1900: "As it is May-day the children were taken into the fields to play this afternoon".

Schoolwork

> Committing to memory, hymns and passages of Scripture [is] particularly desirable for the Infants.

– Inspector's recommendation, 1884.

Infants' Schoolwork

Serious schoolwork began with learning the alphabet and numbers, and then reading, writing and arithmetic. The tools included slates and slate-pencils, steel-nibbed pens and inkwells, and lined writing books with a sentence printed at the top of each page which had to be copied on every line, very carefully. We still use the expression "blotting your copy-book", even though most of us have never seen one.

Lucky children started at an Infants' School, or were taught in a separate classroom. If not, they found themselves in one large classroom with six other classes of older children, all being taught at the same time. An Inspector at Hartington reported in 1877, "The children under seven are backward; as there is no classroom it is extremely difficult for them to be properly instructed". On 21st August 1878 the Head was able to note, " Used the new Classroom for the 1st time".

As the concepts of learning and teaching developed among School Inspectors and teachers, infants began to have a more pleasant school experience. An Inspector at Hartington advised on the Infant Class in 1886: "Marching, Repetition and Action Songs should form a part of the instruction". In 1892 the recommendation was "It would be advisable to introduce some more Occupations". Some of the "occupations" suggested by an Inspector at Melbourne Infants' in 1892 were: for the "babies" coloured balls and string beads, and a K.G. Alphabet (which was quite expensive at 2s.6d. a box); for the 2nd class coloured paper for folding, and individual letters of the alphabet printed on cards, for word-building; for the 1st class embroidery, drawing, mat-plaiting [with strips of paper] and using Dominoes to learn numbers.

There is no doubt that the under-sevens enjoyed these activities, and the teachers welcomed them. At Brimington Common in 1893 the Head commented, "I have been pleased with the brick-building in Infant classes", and in 1894 they started on two new occupations: laying dinner table, and laying tea table; but the Head did not record how successful they were.

The infants also enjoyed the Physical Exercises, marching and 'drill'. There were some drawbacks. The Headmistress of Melbourne Infants', who was fighting off an attack of influenza in February 1890, took a morning off, went into school for the afternoon session, but was "obliged to leave at 3.30 as I could not bear the noise of the marching lesson". She would have sympathised with the Head of Pinxton who noted in 1878, "The boys ... sing heartily, but without skill". And also with the Head at Brimington Common in 1890, who went into "the infant room to listen to Singing and Marching. The former heavy and too loud, & in Marching the children do not keep together in exercises". She also went to check on a Pupil Teacher's work with the Infants, and noted:

> They are just beginning to read out of a book & they spelt out a page nicely. L. Hancock gave a lesson on a cat but the lesson was not simplified sufficiently for little ones.

The cat was not, of course, the school cat or any real cat, but an abstract cat, shown in a picture, which typified cats in general. It was an Object Lesson, which children of four or five met with when they started school and became familiar with throughout their schooldays.

Objects in the Infants' Department at Brimington Common in 1884 included: The Mole, The Elephant, The Cow, The Pig. At Hartington in 1899: Duck, Pig, Camel, Birds – their habits, uses, etc., nests and eggs. Animals – their shape, size, colour, uses &c. The horse, dog, sheep, cow, rabbit. Common objects and materials such as Grass, Hay, Brick, Sugar, Paper, Cork were also regularly used as 'Objects' for lessons. Like the Copy-Book which one must not blot, the Object Lesson has survived in everyday speech as the example from which everyone must learn.

As well as beginning to read and taking part in Object Lessons, Infants had to learn to write and do sums, not always with immediate success. In 1887 the Inspector visiting Melbourne School reported, "Reading and Writing ... fair. The children entirely failed to add or

1

1890

Jany. 12th Commenced entries in a "Teachers
Time Book"

16th Lists of 'Lessons' for next few weeks:

Standard 2

Teacher Jane Hawley (1st Year).

1. Pens.
2. Ink.
3. Cotton.
4. Tea.
5. Linen.
6. Cocoa.
7. Sugar.
8. Jackets.
9. Recap. of Lessons on "Wild Animals"
10. A Book.

Standard 3

Teacher. Mary Allen (3rd Year)

1. Thirst.
2. Eggs.
3. Paper.
4. Products of coal.

2

5. Sir Walter Raleigh
6. Food stuffs containing Starch.
7. Matches.
8. Bone
9. Nuts.
10. Uses of Cotton & Linen.

Standard 4.
Teacher. Ellen Hancock (4th Year).
1. Flies.
2. Exercise
3. Dairy produce.
4. Frost.
5. Honesty.
6. Truth.
7. Food stuffs containing Albumen
8. Cork
9. Rain.
10. Drought.

Standard 5 & 6.
Teacher. Florence Briddon (Asst.)
1. Poultry

Topics for object lessons at Kirkstead Girls School

subtract the easiest numbers…". In 1894 the teachers were warned, "Fingers should not be used in counting". At Brimington Common in 1883 the Head herself examined the Infant Department and noted, "Reading … Chief fault, want of modulation in the voice". An Inspector at Hartington made the same criticism more bluntly: "The reading is rather like chanting".

Scripture or Bible Study also began in school at an early age. In 1884 the Inspector at Hartington advised, "The Infants and Standard I ought to … learn short passages of Scripture and some simple Hymns". Learning off by heart or memorising verses of hymns and passages from the Bible was recommended for the youngest pupils "who otherwise cannot learn much".

Some Infants should have been grateful for an understanding teacher. On 24th November 1893 the Head at Brimington Common

> …altered the time-table in the infant room, shortening the Bible lesson. It seems rather too long to keep infants' attention from 9 to 9.50. It is now from 9 to 9.30.

Putting Bible pictures on the walls also helped children to understand what they had to learn. A Diocesan Inspector at Hartington in May 1879 expressed approval: "The introduction of Scripture prints is a great improvement". In 1885 the Headmistress at Melbourne Infants' recorded, "W. D. Fane Esq. has kindly presented twelve Scripture pictures to be placed on the walls of the school".

Edmond Estcourt, Rector of Eckington, mentioned in his Diary the Scripture lessons and religious education in which he was involved in the early 1860s:

Wednesday 8th February 1860

> Went to the Girls' School and scolded because none of the children except the first Class could say the Catechism.

9th April 1861

> At the Girls' School. Questioned them upon the Creation.

16th April

> Questioned them upon the history of the Patriarchs.

On 8th June he visited another school to examine them:

> The children appeared to me very dull; in fact, ignorant; but I have such an oppressive cold that perhaps it is I that is dull.

The following year in May he was equally honest:

> Had my three classes. They were dull and so was I.

Lessons for Older Children

After about two years as an Infant, at seven a child went up to the Fifth Class, or Standard I. Three or more years of serious schooling now lay ahead, though there were compensations, and not only the possible distant glory of reaching Standard V, VI or VII, and leaving school to get a good job. There were more immediate benefits. As girls got older they could enjoy mothering the little ones, and as boys became more senior they could impress the younger boys and lead them into mischief.

One sign of seniority was that schoolwork began to be done on paper instead of slates. The Head of Pinxton Boys' School noted in October 1876, shortly after taking over the School, "...writing was very imperfect in all except the 1st class..." and in November, "The 2nd class have been kept to slate writing this week as a means of improving the shape of the letters". In 1869 the Head of Hartington thought it important enough to record, "Gave the first class arithmetic and dictation on paper".

Children who were the first in their family, or village, to go to school were impressed by the novelty of some of the things they saw. It is difficult now to appreciate how some of the Hartington children reacted, a month after their school opened, to the delivery of "a Black Board, two Maps and some books". By May 1898 the pupils would have been much more blasé about the arrival of "Writing books, drawing sheets, slates, Pictures, Rulers, Blackboard, &c.". The infants at Melbourne in 1894 were pleased to have new slates "ruled on the three-line system" to improve their writing; they could copy more easily from the blackboard which was also painted with three white lines. Copy-books were also printed with the three-line system.

When most of the class could read and write they started on regular Dictation lessons. In these the teacher, or a senior pupil, read aloud a passage from a book, slowly and carefully, and the class wrote it down. The books used for dictation and for reading lessons, and for learning bits of history or geography might be anything the teacher thought suitable. As mass education spread after 1870, books specially produced for the purpose were available from a new breed of Educational Publishers.

The boys in Standard I of Belper Pottery School in 1886 were given reading and dictation from Blackie's Reading Book, up to page 49, and Chambers' Reading Book, to page 50. Boys in Standard II had to cope with passages from the same books, but up to p.55 and p.61. Standard III boys had Nelson's Reader up to page 79. Standards IV to VII also had separate History and Geography Readers.

The girls at Kirkstead in 1895 used Chambers' Expressive Readers and Cassell's Readable Readers. (Publishers were becoming more market-conscious). At Kirkstead they also used the Royal History Readers and Lamb's Tales from Shakespeare.

As well as dictation, which tested writing and spelling, a good deal of time was spent on Grammar, learning parts of speech, and in the higher standards, doing parsing and analysis. Writing letters, stories, essays or themes were also part of the English lessons.

Arithmetic or 'sums' went from learning numbers and counting in the Infant classes to Simple Addition, Subtraction, Multiplication and Division (in more modern terms: add-ups, take-aways, times and shares – sometimes known in Derbyshire as Guzzinters). Pounds, shillings and pence were, of course, more difficult to get the hang of than the modern decimal system. Times Tables had to be learnt, and the higher Standards had to try to master such things as Long Division, Fractions and Percentages.

Like the Infants, the older children had Object Lessons, but the Objects were more difficult to describe and to understand: making a fire, making a rice pudding, the manufacture of various articles such as pins, needles, soap and candles were for children of nine or ten. "Products of coal" and "Foodstuffs containing albumen" were more advanced. Abstract ideas such as Good Manners, Honesty and Truth were explained by examples. The appearance in the lists of topics at Brimington Common School of "Kindness to Animals" might suggest some immediate need, as, indeed, would "Obedience to Parents and

Teachers" at Melbourne Infants' in 1889.

Children who were not very adept with words or figures might still shine in practical subjects like Needlework or Drawing. In some schools needlework was taken by both girls and boys in the Infant Department, but as other occupations were introduced for Infants it gradually became the rule in the main school for boys to do drawing and girls needlework.

At Hartington from 1868 onwards the girls had sewing every Monday, Wednesday and Thursday, but it was 1891 when the Head noted, "Commence to teach Drawing throughout the School". The same year, in June, at Melbourne Infants, "...Boys are taking drawing instead of needlework this year". At Pinxton the Headmaster recorded in April 1877, "I began to teach drawing and it seems to be popular". And in June he wrote with satisfaction, "The drawing shows that the boys are interested in it, for they work well at it".

The kind of drawing was 'object drawing' in pencil, of cubes, pyramids, cylinders and other regular shapes, calling for careful shading to convey a sense of solidity. There was no use of colour and little variation in the subject, but it was a welcome change, even for those whose efforts were uninspired.

Girls' needlework was more practical in more ways than one. First, it was useful training for future mothers with a family to dress. The Head of Kirkstead Girls' School recorded in detail in her Log, 9th March 1894, the work she planned. Standard IV were cutting out the pieces of cloth for "infant's shirt". Standard V were to cut out "child's chemise" and both lots of articles were then to be made up by the girls in Standard III. Standards VI and VII were to cut out material for "a pinafore with gathers" which would then be sewn up by Standard IV.

Secondly, as the School provided the materials for the sewing lessons, when the articles were finished, and had been seen by the Inspector, they were sold to help School funds. At Brimington Common on 11th June 1890 there was a "Sale of garments made by children this evening from 5 to 8 o'clock". A Sale at Kirkstead in May 1892 brought in about £7. In May 1895 the Head recorded, "Sale of garments has realised £13.3.4. All the garments are sold except five. There are also a few knitted articles left". This was a considerable sum of money, about as much as a year's school fees for a class of twenty children paying 4d. a week.

Homework

Children starting school, or going up from the Infants may have felt proud at first at being given a little homework to do, but as the amount increased many saw it as a burden to be avoided if at all possible. At Pinxton Boys' School where, in November 1876, "Home lessons were worked willingly", by the following February "several have been kept in during the week for careless Home lessons". At Hartington on 19th May 1869 the Head "Gave the third class some multiplication tables to learn for Home lessons". And on 25th May he "Kept several children in to complete their home lessons". In March 1871 he "Gave the first two classes a letter to write for a home lesson", but there were also frequent cases of "neglect of home lessons".

Many children found it difficult to do homework, especially written work, even if they were willing. It might not be easy to find a steady table to sit at, in a quiet well-lit room; boys might be needed to help with livestock, or to fetch water; girls especially had household tasks to be done and younger children to look after. It was also probable that until late in the nineteenth century the parents had little or no schooling themselves and could not help, even with the most elementary work.

An aspect of school which had much greater appeal to children was when they were told to carry the benches out into the playground on a sunny day, for lessons in the open air. In May 1867 the Head of Hartington noted, "Children taught in the playground part of each day". In June 1877 the Head of Pinxton Boys recorded, "...owing to the great heat the children were listless. I have adopted the plan of putting the reading classes outdoors and found it answers well". Even more enjoyable to some was when a sudden thunderstorm sent everyone rushing back indoors in a glorious scramble of bodies, benches and books.

Poetry, Music and Drama

Children who went to Board Schools discovered early on that their education was not strictly practical. They also learnt and recited poetry and sang songs. Some parents thought that this was a waste of time, and some children did not respond well, especially if too many lines had to be learnt "off by heart". Sometimes, however, even the most unimaginative child could be moved by a poetic description of a familiar scene or by the dramatic declamation of some heroic deed.

Many songs and poems were rather mundane and moralistic. At Brimington Common in 1882 the Infants' recitation pieces included "The dirty girl, or child who did not like to be washed" and "Who stole the bird's nest?". The girls learned to sing "Whatever be our earthly lot". In 1883 "The Wreck of the Hesperus" was learnt for recitation, and the 1885 poems and songs included "Truthfulness", "The Village Blacksmith", "Two Little Kittens" and "My Mother's Picture". In 1891 the choice was more militaristic. Standard I and II learnt "The Battle of Blenheim" and Standards III, IV and V learnt "The Battle of Flodden".

At Hartington in the 1870s and '80s the older children learnt

A school play at Ashover

93

"Hurrah, Hurrah for England", "Work for the Night is Coming" and "Evening Bells". The Infants stayed with nursery rhymes such as "Sing a Song of Sixpence" and "Little Jack Horner", which they sang at the December Concert in aid of School funds. "The Village Blacksmith" was also a favourite at Hartington in the '80s, when, of course, there was a village blacksmith, so the poem was topical rather than nostalgic. Other poems to be recited were "Bruce and the Spider", "The Deserted Village", "The Burial of Sir John Moore" and "Casablanca" ("The Boy Stood on the Burning Deck").

The older boys at Pinxton in 1882 had a rather more difficult task. The 5th Standard were learning Gray's "Elegy in a Country Churchyard", and the 6th and 7th Standards were struggling with speeches from Shakespeare's "Julius Caesar". The older girls at Kirkstead were also 'doing' "Julius Caesar" in 1896, and had to learn Act III Scene II and part of Act IV Scene III. (These were probably the same passages as the Pinxton Boys were learning in 1882. The first is "Friends, Romans, Countrymen" and the second, "There is a tide in the affairs of men...").

Most of the poems and songs came from collections specially published for schools. The boys at Belper Pottery School included in their repertoire "Canadian Boat Song", "The British Grenadiers" and "Rule Britannia", which they sang when the Chairman of the School Board came to visit the school in May 1882. Were these, perhaps, the same songs that the Head of Pinxton Boys' School heard his pupils singing in 1878, which moved him to record in his Log Book, "heartily, but without skill"?

Songs, poems and bits of Shakespeare had more than educational value. The tradition began to grow, towards the end of the 19th century, of having a School Concert some time before Christmas. On 17th December 1890 the Head of Melbourne Infants' wrote, "A little of the schooltime has been taken up this week in the afternoons, in rehearsing for the children's annual school entertainment, the proceeds of which provide prizes for the children". By 1898 this was being held in the Public Hall and ran for two nights.

A more modest show was offered by Brimington Common in December 1896:

Today several mothers and friends of the children in the Infants'

Room came at 3 o'clock & saw drill, games, etc.

This may have been because they had acquired, on 16th June, a "Piano provided by the Board" following an Inspector's remark that "A musical instrument would be of much use".

Kirkstead girls were among the most ambitious performers:

> The teachers and scholars of this school gave a concert on the evening of 27th Dec. [1895; repeated on 29th] ...songs, recitations, drill, &c. [and also] an operetta – The Fairy Chain.

These entertainments raised £11.10s.0d. for school funds. In February 1900 the school had a special two-day holiday to get the room ready for a concert "in aid of the Boys' Brigade & the School prize Fund". It is nice to know that in March 1901 the boys responded in gentlemanly fashion, donating £1 from the Boys' Brigade to the School prize Fund.

Rewards and Punishments

> This boy gives more trouble than any other child in the School.

– Headmaster, on a pupil who had been "using bad language in the Class Room".

Progress, Fast or Slow

Promotion and demotion from one class to another could be regarded as reward or punishment, or merely as matching the level of study to the capability of the child. "Putting up, or down" could take place at any time of the year. At Hartington in February 1870 Adolphus Lomas and Isaac Belfield were both put up a class, though the Log does not mention why. In May 1898 a new Headmaster grumbled, "Only three infants know their letters" and added, referring to other classes, "Promoted the scholars to their new Standards but many of them are unfit for promotion". (New Head Teachers usually complained about the poor state of the school they were taking over).

It was normal for most pupils to go up into the next Standard every year, but at Kirkstead, for example, in 1890 the Headmistress put fourteen girls up one Standard for a trial period of three months and demoted seventeen. In some cases a pupil worked with one class for most subjects, but in a lower class for one subject. This happened at Brimington Common, for instance, in 1891, when three girls were moved from Standard IV down to Standard III "for Arithmetic only".

Sometimes a pupil failed to keep up with the rest of the class because of having missed lessons. At Kirkstead in September 1892

> Mary Hancock, one of seven girls promoted to St. III has been put back into St. II in consequence of irregular attendance. [S. A. Broomhead, at Hartington in 1889 was] through continued ill health, placed in the infants class on readmission, not being able to proceed with the 1st Standard.

In other cases, children were simply unable to go beyond a certain level as their classmates of the same age moved up. No doubt many of the teachers were sympathetic, but some of their comments in the Log Books now seem unacceptably blunt. Mary S- "not able to keep up with her standard, being deficient in intellect"; Frances A- "excessively dull"; Hannah and Ellen S- "unmistakably dull, and unable to keep up with the others".

To save the feelings of a big girl or boy having to sit and work with seven- or eight-year-olds, a Head Teacher sometimes disregarded normal practice. So, the Headmistress at Kirkstead wrote in January 1889:

> Linda C- has been admitted on the Standard III register, she is a big girl, but of weak intellect and sits with the older girls, though unable to do their work.

Misbehaviour, Truancy and Rudeness

Accidents will happen – but someone has got to pay! It was usually boys who were responsible for breakages. Hartington, February 1867: "One of the windows broken by football ... Scholars subscribed towards repairing it". May 1871: "Isaac Percival, Wm. Grindon, John Naden and Wm. Stone broke the cast iron plate on the school door, and were required to pay 6d. each to replace it". 1873: "James Peach and Thomas Gibbs broke one of the cast iron pegs in the cloke room – value 3d."

If parents refused to pay, strong action could be taken, as at South Normanton in June 1881:

> The Clerk [of the School Board] was directed to write to Raymond Rowe requiring him to pay 1s.6d. for the breaking of a window ... by his son Arthur Rowe and to inform him that if such sum were not paid on or before the 14th inst., legal proceedings would be taken.

At times, for reason or another, children were late for school, or absent without good cause, and they were punished – though not always caned, though "punishment" usually meant "caning". At Hartington in September 1867 T. Bentley was "punished severely for playing truant, it being his second offence". A fortnight later, two girls were punished "by task" for being absent without permission. (A task usually meant extra work). In January 1869 the Head "Kept the late children in during play time" and in April "Kept the late children in 20 minutes" (at going home time, of course).

Children found it hardest to resist the lure of the lanes and fields in the Summer Term. At Hartington on 31st August 1869 James Pickford was caned "for playing truant on Monday afternoon". A

Ashover School – some didn't keep still

few days later William Grindon and Isaac Belfield were kept in "till six o'clock for playing in the streets instead of coming to school". Later in the 19th century most School Boards did not allow children to be kept in later than five o'clock. The requirement of a note from parents to explain lateness or absence could not, of course, be enforced until most parents were able to write.

Infants were rarely absent or late without obvious causes such as illness or bad weather. One case recorded in Melbourne on 29th June 1894 concerned two little six-year-olds, David Robey and John Crane, who arrived at school at 10.15, over an hour late: "so they were punished with the cane, as I found they had been playing in the fields".

Many children misbehaved in lessons, through talking, inattention or worse. This is all the more understandable when we consider that lessons were not always very interesting, and their 'teachers' were commonly older children acting as monitors or pupil-teachers, who could be as young as fourteen. Frequent references occur in Log Books: "Kept Samuel Naden in for inattention", "...kept in for copying during dictation lesson", "Punished George Brown for inattention". All these at Hartington, 1868-1869. Annie Nottingham was punished at Brimington Common in 1889 "for copying an answer to a sum & repeatedly denying it afterwards. She had the right answer but by wrong working". A not uncommon phenomenon!

More serious was deliberate disobedience and rudeness. Isaac Belfield and Frank Smith of Hartington were both caned for disobedience in January 1870. In September 1885 R. Bradbury was caned "for disobedience and gross insubordination". At Brimington Common in August 1884 Hilda Hayes was punished for disobedience in the Pupil Teacher's class. Bad behaviour could also be found in the Infants' class there. On 4th November 1895 the Head noted, "Have sent Richard Yates home this afternoon for extreme rudeness and disobedience to his teachers". We can only speculate on his reception at home on the basis of the next day's entry in the Log: "I have allowed R. Yates to come back as he has promised to obey". The case had no lasting effect on others, however. The following July, Sam and Luther Neale were both sent home "for Excessive rudeness & disobedience".

Children in the playground or otherwise unsupervised often behaved badly. Boys were the usual offenders: fighting, throwing stones (not necessarily at each other), bullying younger boys and writing on walls – one of the undesirable results of literacy!

At Hartington in August 1870, William Stone, Edward Broomhead and Isaac Belfield were kept in for 45 minutes for throwing stones. In October 1873 the Head "caned John Gibbs for throwing stones in the playground after being cautioned about it". At Brimington in May 1884 three boys in the Infant Department were punished for stone-throwing.

At Hartington in October 1873 George Brown was caned "for ill-using one of the little ones in the play ground" and in February 1875 Alfred Pickford was caned "for quarrelling and fighting". In September 1880 the head of Pottery Boys' School in Belper recorded, "Punished William Wood and Robert Hardy for fighting in Class Room, cut Wood's thumb slightly with cane". A potentially very dangerous incident happened in the same school in May 1879. The Head noted:

> Severely punished Thomas Taylor, a First Class lad, for frightening a little boy in the Third Class, by threatening to cut his throat; he had actually, with a pocket knife, made a mark across the little boy's neck.

Writing or using bad language was always severely punished, but without any lasting result. In November 1870 George Wain of Hartington was "punished for swearing", but then, unusually, was "taken away from school" by his parents in protest. In 1875 an Inspector's Report concluded "Discipline good ... work fairly done", but added "...writing on the walls of the offices [toilets] must be put a stop to". About a week later the Head recorded in the Log Book, "The Offices Whitewashed".

Belper Pottery School had a number of such troublesome boys. George Wain (not the same one) was punished on 13th November 1878 "for writing bad language on the School Walls". A month later William Milward was punished "for writing obscene language on his slate". The following April Anthony Stone and William Oliver were caned "for writing on the School Walls". George Wain was again in trouble in November 1880 "for using bad language in the playground". In January 1881 Charles Whewell was beaten "for using bad language in Class Room", having already been punished earlier in the day "for talking, playing, and being excessively troublesome". The Head concluded in his Log Book, "This boy gives more trouble than any other child in the School".

On occasions girls could prove troublesome too, though not usually for using or writing bad language. Headmistresses, however, could be formidable opponents, who generally had the last word. One girl who discovered this was Daisy Riley, in the Fifth Standard at Kirkstead School in September 1892.

One Tuesday, having been "a continual source of annoyance to her teacher" she was caned by the Head. When playtime came she went home and "her mother refused to allow her to come back". On Wednesday her mother went to complain to the Chairman of the School Board, who said that there were no grounds for complaint and that Daisy would have to go to school. When she returned to school on Thursday the Headmistress recorded, "I have punished her for the second offence – that of leaving school during school hours without permission – with three stripes of the cane on her hands".

Prizes, Treats and Outings

Rewards came in two sorts: the individual prize for the 'good' child, and the collective 'treat' to encourage all pupils. Prizes generally meant books – 'reward books' – and were mainly given for punctuality, regular attendance and good behaviour.

At Melbourne Infants', on 13th November 1891, "Miss Fane visited the school this morning, with her little nephew who is going to India. The children sang and recited... Sweets were afterwards distributed by Miss Fane". In 1894 prizes were given out on 10th May and "Mrs. Thompson kindly sent sweets to be given to the children". In July 1896, on closing for Summer Holiday, "Through the kindness of Mrs. Knipe each child received a packet of sweets".

Sometimes the treat was more than just sweets. In January 1896, when the school re-opened after Christmas, the Infants found that Mr. Armson had given them "a safety rocking-horse" for the "baby room ... a great attraction for the little ones", as the Headmistress recorded. She herself was so delighted that she made the entry in the School Log in red ink!

Another unusual 'treat' at Melbourne was perhaps less welcome to the children, though undoubtedly "good for" them. On 23rd November 1898, with only 33 pupils present out of 143 because of a snowstorm, "Mrs. Singleton has been exceedingly kind, and ... sent a large bottle of cough mixture to be given to the children with colds".

A tea-party, or 'tea-drinking', was often held to entertain schoolchildren. Rev. Edmond Estcourt of Eckington noted a tea-drinking in his Diary in February 1860. It was at Mosbrough School:

> 69 children present. Allowed tea and plum cake ad lib. After they had finished they went out to play while we had tea; Upon their re-admission each child had two halves of an orange. [Why two halves?]

On Whit Monday 1862 there was a joint party for Eckington and Mosbrough children:

> We had 800 buns made by Parker. Sarah Billam made the Spice Cake, 30lbs., for the children's tea. It was excellent.

At Brimington Common there were "prizes for regular attendance" on 1st August 1889. "45 prizes were distributed by Members of the Board... There was a good attendance of parents, being an evening distribution". On 18th February 1890 there was a surprise. Mr. Ashmore visited the school and "kindly gave each child in school an orange".

The First Class boys at Hartington in May 1869 were allowed to take home the maps of Palestine which they had drawn. In 1880 a book was awarded "as a prize for Cleanliness and general good Behaviour". In 1882 eight girls were given prizes "for proficiency in Needlework", and in 1898 "Reward Cards", in effect certificates, were being given for regular attendance.

In September 1891 Kirkstead Girls' School started a new prize scheme, with marks being given for punctuality, attendance and conduct. A general treat was planned in July 1895 for the girls to have a trip to Hardwick Hall, which was, in due course, "thoroughly enjoyed by all concerned". They had another outing in August 1897, to "the Monument Recreation Grounds, Codnor Park".

Parental Worries

> ...the Boys use the Girls' yard as a Water-closet and behave in other unseemly ways.

– Headmistress on the need for segregation.

Lack of Heating

Heating in school was a problem for everyone – parents, teachers and children. It was costly, troublesome and generally ineffective, being achieved in most schools before 1900 by open fires, or enclosed stoves which were safer but less efficient. The children suffered most. Thirty, forty or more could not all sit within the heating range of a fire. The clever ones, at the top of the class, near the teacher's desk, were also nearest the source of heat.

Fires were usually started in mid-October or early November and were stopped in early to mid-April, depending on the weather. Sometimes they had to be started again, as at Hartington in April 1873. On 15th the Log recorded, "Fires discontinued", but on 25th "had fires ... on Thursday and Friday, the weather being very cold". In 1891, on 29th May the Head noted, "had fires in the School all the week in consequence of the cold weather".

Parents often complained about cold schools and sometimes took direct action. At Hartington in 1871 the Head noted on 1st December, "Several children left owing to complaints of the room being cold". On 15th February 1888 the Head at Brimington Common wrote:

> Attendance very poor today ... owing to a deep snow. I sent in an application for more heating apparatus in my school for I find my school intensely cold and this interferes both with the work & health of both teachers & scholars; to which application I received the following reply. 'The managers do not think it necessary to make any further provision for warming your school'. [But in

January she noted] A stove has been placed in Infant room that has made it very warm & comfortable.

As well as being inefficient at heating a large room, open fires tended to be sensitive to the type of fuel being used and to the force and direction of the wind. Teachers got very upset by this, as did mothers who had to wash smoky, sooty clothes. For children it could be an exciting diversion from schoolwork, and sometimes it meant an unexpected holiday:

Brimington Common School. 7th December 1882.

The fire in the girls' room would not draw at all. The smoke poured down the whole morning. I was obliged to close the school & send for the sweep this afternoon to see if that would improve it.

24th January 1883.

The fire in the Infant Department blew straight out, the smoke & soot filling the room. The Infants were sent home in the afternoon.

12 February 1883.

I have been obliged to close the school for smoke again today. The rooms were a scene of dense smoke.

Melbourne Infants' also suffered from inefficient heating. In December 1892 a visiting Inspector commented, "Room not sufficiently warmed. Thermometer needed". On 13th February 1895 the Head noted, "Stove altered to increase heat". And a week later, "The room is very much warmer". But a year later, in February 1896, "thermometer only reached 50 degrees at the opening of school every morning this week". On 6th November, "a little over 40 degrees this morning". (These figures, of course, are in degrees Fahrenheit).

Children at Hartington School were even worse off. On 26th February 1896 the temperature at 9 o'clock was only 35 degrees. On 27th January 1897 at 1.25 p.m. it was 49 degrees and did not reach 50 until 3.20. In the following year, on 25th February it was only 39 degrees at 9 a.m. Not surprisingly, in March an Inspector reported, "New stoves needed".

Dirt of one sort and another

Heating, or the lack of it, was not the only hardship which children had to endure and parents had to worry about. Anxiety might be caused by other children, who came to school with head lice, ringworm and other contagious conditions, or who might lead others astray into bad language and bad habits.

In July 1882, after the summer holiday, the Head of Belper Pottery Boys' School was taken aback by William Spencer's mother, who

> ...informed me that her boy had left this school because the majority of children in attendance were so very rough & dirty, & she objected to her child mixing with them.

There were other worries too, but parents had to rely on the Head to address them. The playground might be unsafe. An Inspector at Brimington Common in 1885 reported:

> The drain in the playground is stopped [blocked] and the playground itself is so rough with broken pieces of asphalt that it is dangerous.

Boys and girls had to be kept apart when not in lessons, either by letting them out to play at different times or by having separate yards, so that the boys could indulge in their boisterous games without upsetting the girls. In 1876 the Head at Hartington noted, "The communication between the boys' and girls' playgrounds closed, by recommendation of Mr. Blandford, H.M.I."

Open access between playgrounds could lead to worse offences, as the Headmistress at Kirkstead recorded in October 1890:

> The want of a gate between the Boys' and Girls' playgrounds has caused, during the last three months, great annoyance. This has been reported three times and still the Boys use the Girls' yard as a Water-closet & behave in other unseemly ways on our premises. Yesterday, I found five boys in the Girls' Closets.

Further concern to the Head, and parents, was the ineffective fence "between the girls' offices and the adjoining allotments" in 1898, which had to be "replaced by a wall or close fence". She also referred to a phenomenon, fairly commonly noticed in schools, usually in hot weather, but on this occasion on 23rd November 1894:

> Placed some disinfecting fluid about the school as there were some rather unpleasant smells in it, owing to its overcrowded state, notwithstanding all the ventilators were open.

The provision and state of cloakrooms was another problem which grew as time passed, and children were sent to school in outdoor clothing in bad weather instead of simply being kept at home. Some schools had no cloakrooms. At Brimington Common in March 1894 an Inspector told the Head, "All clothes should be kept out of the [school] room", and she was to enquire whether the Board would "provide sufficient cloak room accommodation". The Head of Kirkstead Girls' School asked her School Boards to put gas-light in the cloakroom, in December 1895:

> ...as, when school is dismissed in the afternoon it is so dark as to be quite impossible for the girls to see their hats &c., and this causes confusion.

[Or was this just a good excuse for a bit of larking about?]

Cleaning of schools was also something which improved as time went on, to the benefit of the pupils' health and the state of their clothes. Whitewashing or "colouring" the walls was done when they looked as if they needed it, and sweeping of floors and dusting

Edward Revell Endowed School, Hallfield Gate

tended to be perfunctory. In 1894 the Head of Kirkstead Girls' School complained:

> The school is in a very dirty condition. Although the pictures were taken down from the walls so that they might be swept, the caretaker has not touched them and the dust lies thickly on the ledges of the bricks.

She and many earlier teachers would have been very envious of the state of the schools in the care of the Belper School Board in 1886, as set out in its Regulations.

In Winter, fires were to be "banked up at night so as to maintain the circulation of warm water in the pipes". "In hot weather" all windows were to be opened "before the admission of the children and after they have left". There was to be "all the year round, an even temperature of from 55 to 60 degrees". All furniture was to be dusted daily, "not later than 7.40 a.m." and all rooms and passages were to be swept every afternoon. The caretaker was also to see "that the conveniences are clean" and to "clear the yards and playgrounds of dirt, paper and rubbish". Various other cleaning routines were specified to be done weekly or quarterly, and the half-yearly job was "to wash the schoolroom and classroom floors, maps, furniture, etc."

Glossary to Part I

Parlour boarder – a pupil who 'lived in' almost as a member of his tutor's family.

Erasmus Darwin – less well-known grandfather of Charles Darwin, author of "The Origin of Species".

Washed out – their clothes sent out of the school to be washed by a laundry or washerwoman.

Trowes – trousers.

Fustians – thick cotton cloth.

Aff. or affte. – affectionate

Going down – going home at the end of term.

Going up – going to boarding school.

Beresford...Cotton – Beresford Dale, near Ashbourne, and the small house of Charles Cotton, the "Izaak Walton" of Derbyshire.

Hall Well – referring to the Derbyshire custom of Well-Dressing.

Amusing – not 'funny' but 'interesting'.

Accidence – variations in forms of words.

Hic concludam...etc – "Here I end my letter, you will be worn out (with reading it)".

Calisthenics – "keep fit" exercises suitable for ladies.

Hoops – a hoop was a large ring of wood or metal. A boy would roll it beside him as he ran along.

Wordsworth – the well-known poet.

Dunned – hounded by a debt collector.

Fag – a younger boy who has to obey the orders of a senior; to fag someone – to treat as a fag.

Morris-tube – a narrow metal tube fitted into the barrel of a gun to make it possible to use small bullets for target practice.

Swell voluntaries – solos to be played on an organ: Richard may be having a joke. The "swell pedal" on an organ is used to make it louder, but "swell" could also mean, in the slang sense, "great" or "brilliant".

Pelisse – a long cloak.

Epaulets – decorative frills worn on the shoulders of a coat.

Beaver hat – hat made of beaver fur.

Gruel – watery soup.

Bread & scrape – a slice of bread very thinly buttered.

Gudgeon – a small fish, sometimes used as live bait.

In terrorem – Latin, meaning "to terrify" the others.

Fagues – alternative spelling of "fags".

Drugget – coarse woollen carpet.

Tetter – a spot or pimple.

Pottle of strawberries – a little basket of strawberries.

Currain tart – currant tart.

A black dose – cascara or other laxative.

The Sick Cottage – a separate building where seriously ill pupils could have medical treatment and an appropriate diet. It also avoided the infection of other pupils.

Glossary to Part 2

Forms – wooden benches.

Quire – 24 sheets of paper.

Quill – a pen made from the large wing feather of a large bird, usually a goose, sharpened to a point.

Inkstand – a wooden box to hold a small cup, the inkwell which held the ink for a "dipping" pen.

Slate pencil – a stick made of compressed, powdered slate. It was used for writing on a slate. The words could be wiped off with a damp cloth.

Numberless appliances – these would include such things as wooden bricks with letters or numbers on each side, and beads of different colours strung on wires fixed in a wooden frame. These bead-frames were used in teaching children to count.

A great desideratum – something badly needed.

Catechism – a series of questions and answers used in teaching religion.

Copy book – This was used to practise writing. A line was printed at the top of each page in "copperplate" this is, it looked as if it had been written. This had to be copied on every line down the page. The words to be copied were usually a saying, such as "Evil doers never prosper" or "Make hay while the sun shines".

Ribbands – ribbons.

Review – a military parade by the local volunteers – part-time soldiers.

A K.G. alphabet – K.G. = kindergarten – the "babies" class.

The Three-line system – pages of the copybook were printed with three lines. Short letters such as a, c or m had to fit between lines one and two. Capital letters and tall letters like t or l had to touch the top line.

ALSO PUBLISHED BY SCARTHIN BOOKS

DERBYSHIRE CHURCHES AND CHAPELS OPEN TO VISITORS

Compiled by Rodney Tomkins, Illustrated by Elisabeth Stoppard, foreword by the Bishop of Derby

Illustrated paperback   128 pages   ISBN 1 900446 02 2

TRANSFORMATION OF A VALLEY: THE DERBYSHIRE DERWENT

By Brian Cooper, photographs by Neville Cooper

Illustrated hardback   328 pages   ISBN 0 907758 17 7

THE HISTORY OF THE DERBYSHIRE GENERAL INFIRMARY 1810–1894

By V.M. Leveaux, foreword by Jeremy Taylor

Illustrated cloth-bound hardback 160 pages   ISBN 1 900446 006

THE DIARIES OF MARIA GYTE OF SHELDON DERBYSHIRE 1913–1920

Edited by Gerald Phizackerley, foreword by His Grace the Duke of Devonshire

Illustrated paperback   332 pages + 16 pages of plates
                                                        ISBN 0 907758 96 7

HANGED FOR A SHEEP: CRIME IN BYGONE DERBYSHIRE

By E.G. Power

Illustrated paperback   80 pages   ISBN 0 907758 00 2

HISTORIC ORGANS IN DERBYSHIRE: A SURVEY FOR THE MILLENNIUM

By Rodney Tomkins, foreword by Nicholas Thistlewaite

Illustrated cloth-bound hardback 304 pages   ISBN 0 907758 97 5

THE HOSPITALLER ORDER OF ST. JOHN OF JERUSALEM IN DERBYSHIRE HISTORY

By *Gladwyn Turbutt*

Illustrated cloth-bound hardback 64 pages ISBN 1 900446 01 4

ST. JOHN'S CHAPEL, BELPER: THE LIFE OF A CHURCH AND A COMMUNITY

By *E.G. Power*

Illustrated paperback 40 pages ISBN 0 907758 11 8

A STAGE OR TWO BEYOND CHRISTENDOM: A SOCIAL HISTORY OF THE CHURCH OF ENGLAND IN DERBYSHIRE

By *Michael Austen*

350 pages + 24 pages Illustration (some colour)
paperback: ISBN 1 900446 03 0
cloth-bound hardback: ISBN 0 1 900446 04 9

DERBYSHIRE IN THE CIVIL WAR

By *Brian Stone*

Illustrated hardback 157 pages, with notes, bibliography and index
ISBN 0 907758 58 4

DERBYSHIRE CHILDREN AT HOME 1800–1900

By *E.G. Power*

Illustrated paperback 90 pages ISBN 1 900446 057

http://www.scarthinbooks.com